YORKSHIRE'S CHRISTMAS

YORKSHIRE'S CHRISTMAS

compiled by David Joy

A DALESMAN ANTHOLOGY

The Dalesman Publishing Company Ltd,
Clapham, Lancaster, LA2 8EB

First published 1992

© Dalesman Publishing Company Ltd, 1992

ISBN: 1 85568 050 9

Illustrations

Colour illustrations by John Edenbrow (page 33), Ionicus (34 and 69), Clifford Robinson (36 and 71), Mack (70) and William Bennett (72). Line drawings in the text by D. Binns, Will Clemence, Ian M. Emberson, A. Bell Foster, Marie Hartley, Ionicus, E. Jeffrey, Fred Lawson, Rowland Lindup, L. Robinson, John Selby, Alec Wright, Victoria Wright and other *Dalesman* artists.

Typeset by Lands Services, East Molesey, Surrey
Printed and bound by Biddles of Guildford, Surrey

CONTENTS

1. CHRISTMASES PAST   7

2. CUSTOMS OF YESTERYEAR   25

3. CHRISTMAS SHOPPING   32

4. GREETINGS!   41

5. CHRISTMAS DECORATIONS   46

6. SEASONAL FARE   54

7. CHILDHOOD DAYS   63

8. CHRISTMAS MUSIC   71

9. ON THE FARM   81

10. GHOSTLY ENCOUNTERS   89

11. TODAY'S CHRISTMAS   95

1

CHRISTMASES PAST

IN THE BEGINNING

Yorkshire, it seems, can claim credit for being the home of the first Christmas festivities ever held in Britain. When, in 521, King Arthur won the Battle of Baddan Hills, he took up his winter quarters in the city of York and kept the festival of Christmas Day there. The rejoicings lasted for 12 days and appealed strongly to the population of the city. The idea spread quickly to other parts of the country and became an accepted part of the season.

(1954)

MID-VICTORIAN TIMES

To many of us *A Christmas Carol*, Charles Dickens' book, is essential December reading. And each time I read it, I think particularly of "The Ghost of Christmas Past", who recalled his boyhood days to Ebeneezer Scrooge. Inevitably, my thoughts go back to the years of the eighteen-sixties when Dickens was still alive; what a story he could have written of Christmas in Yorkshire. Certainly, Christmas 1869 in these parts provided much that would have delighted him.

One of the proudest men in Yorkshire that Christmas was Farmer John Outhwaite of Bainesse, near Catterick. He had not only won first prize for his great bullock at the London Cattle Show, with a cash award of £30, but afterwards sold the beast to a London butcher for £75. Moreover, he had gained two "firsts" and a prize of a further £20 at the Leeds show. He had also brought home a celebration poem:

> And here's our friend John Outhwaite,
> May his shadow never grow less,
> As he strides among the green crops,
> And the green land of Bainesse.
> Above a first prize bullock,
> Appears the welcome "Sold",
> Right well he knows the way to turn
> His turnips into gold.

On St. Thomas's Day (December 21) Christmas poultry and pigs went the same way as Mr. Outhwaite's fat ox, for this was the day they were slaughtered in accordance with the ancient couplet:

> On St. Thomas the Divine
> Kill all turkeys, geese and swine.

To many of the poor, however, it was best known as the day on which charitable gifts were distributed. In many places this was called the "St. Thomas's Day Dole". At Holbeck, almost five hundred people received gifts that day under the terms of Metcalfe's Charity. Altogether the churchwardens handed out lengths of calico which totalled eleven hundred yards, 36 pairs of blankets, 20 coverlets, 20 pairs of cotton sheets and 80 flannel petticoats.

A few days earlier, £50 was given out to residents of Shipley, Windhill and Saltaire. Each year this sum was received by Mr. Jesse Cockshutt and Mr. Edward Brumfit from a former Shipley man who would not disclose his name. At Sheffield a resident gave a half-pound packet of tea to two thousand less fortunate citizens, and in the village of Queensbury, near Bradford, Messrs. John Foster and Son made very sure there were fires for poor widows and old folk, for they sent round 50 cart-loads of coal and 40 pairs of blankets to humble homes.

At Holbeck, where poor widows got the flannel petticoats on St. Thomas's Day, there was a special event on Christmas Eve — a canary-singing concert at the *King William Inn*. Thirteen birds competed for the Christmas prizes and the winner was a fine vocalist owned by Mr. James Worshop, of Wortley. Meanwhile, at the North Riding Asylum at Clifton, there was singing of a different kind. A choir hailed Christmas Day by going round the wards at midnight carolling "O come, all ye faithful". If some of the patients were a little disgruntled at having musical visitors at such a late hour, no doubt they were mollified by the lavish Christmas dinner, washed down by a half-pint of ale, which was served to them a few hours later.

Was it really the happiest day of the year at the workhouse? It certainly appeared to be so at York, for in the workhouse there the 430 inmates disposed of "50 stones of prime roast beef" and went on to tackle what were described as "35 monster plum puddings".

There was another traditional dinner in Leeds, where the 5th Dragoon Guards were barracked. They dined at the expense of their officers, in rooms whose walls were smothered with flags. After dinner many hundreds of civilians, including a great number of pretty young ladies, thronged to the barracks to be the soldiers' guests for the rest of the day. Then there was a grand dance to martial music.

Much of the carol-singing on Christmas Day was provided by Methodists. Those of the village of High Farndale in the North Riding honoured a custom which had sent John Wesley's followers round the neighbourhood for several decades. When they arrived at Mr. William Featherstone's home they found that dinner awaited them. After several more hours of singing in the afternoon they finished up at Mrs. Foord's home for a Christmas tea. A party of about 130 young Methodists from Arkendale sang in nearby Arkletown, touring the farms in procession, led by a young stalwart who carried a flag.

North Frodingham, near Driffield, had a party of Christmas waits who sang round the district to get money for a feast for the widows and widowers of the parish. They were not connected with any particular church or denomination, but obviously had the support of the best singers of the parish church and the chapels as well. In addition to getting money, they received gifts such as poultry and pigs. The meal made possible by their efforts in 1869 included roast beef, hares, geese and ham.

Driffield seems to have been the first of the Yorkshire towns to announce that it would also observe December 27 as a holiday: Christmas Day fell on a Saturday in 1869. The tradesmen proposed to close their premises until the Tuesday morning, "to allow those in their employ the opportunity of visiting distant friends" and they went on to express the hope that their plan "would be adopted by every town in the United Kingdom". No doubt some people did spend the holiday with "distant friends", but the majority preferred to find their entertainment near at hand. There was much snow and ice over the three days, and poor widows were doubly glad of their Christmas blankets.

In the cities, the chief attraction on the Monday was the pantomime. There was a large attendance at the Theatre Royal in Leeds for *Robinson Crusoe*, or *Friday and the Fairies*, but the most appreciative audience of all was at a special morning performance on New Year's Day, when all seats were free. It was made up of elderly people from Leeds workhouse, the children of the Industrial School, and the boys from Holbeck workhouse. All attended under an annual custom observed by the manager, Mr. Coleman. He also gave the old folk a glass of ale and the youngsters a plum bun.

Clifford Morsley (1970)

LITERARY CHRISTMASES

The season of Christmas has always been a favourite subject with writers of fiction. Mrs. Gaskell, a happy housewife and mother, revelled in Christmas gaieties, and in *Sylvia's Lovers* she depicts with the pen of a true home lover Mrs. Corney and her daughters preparing for a Christmas party in their Yorkshire farmhouse. The guests romped noisily through all the old north country games – "Turn the Trencher", "Blind Man's Buff", "Forfeits", and "Hunt the Slipper". They then sat down to a substantial meal of spiced beef and plum cake, washed down with beer that was only moderately strong, so that the men could drink plenty, and yet not "spoil the fun", as Mrs. Corney concisely expressed it. The supper was very friendly and informal, with plenty of squeezing and sitting together on chairs.

Charlotte Brontë's description in *Jane Eyre* of a Yorkshire Christmas at Gateshead Hall was purely that of an onlooker. It is probable that this shy little genius had never in her life taken part in a Christmas romp, and would be at a loss to describe one. Very likely she was recalling her own experiences as a governess when she writes: "From every enjoyment I was, of course, excluded. My share consisted to watching the daily apparelling of Eliza and Georgina, and seeing them descend to the drawing room decked out in muslim frocks and scarlet sashes with hair most elaborate ringleted, and in listening to the sound of the harp or the piano played below, or the jingling of glass and china as refreshments were handed, while I sat in the dark silent nursery." Later on, when Jane comes into her fortune, she spends Christmas Day "house cleaning and cake making".

J.B. Priestley, in one of his best-known books, *Bright Day,* gives a delightful description of a Christmas in a Yorkshire industrial town before the First World War. "Christmas in those day was far less of a commercial racket to boost the winter trade, but more a hearty and widespread enjoyment of the

11

season itself. Brass bands played and carols were sung in the streets. You visited dozens of houses where rich cakes and mince pies were washed down with beer and port, whiskey and rum, the air was fragrant and thick with cigar smoke, whole warehouses of presents were exchanged, and shops overflowed with turkeys, geese, hams, puddings, candied fruit, figs, dates, chocolate, holly and coloured or gilded paper hats. There was been nothing like it since, and probably will not be again. We Yorkshire people celebrated Christmas in a huge rich leisurely way."

M.L. Stollard (1967)

CHRISTMAS AT BATTY WIFE HOLE

(An imaginary visit to the most famous – and notorious – shanty town on the Settle-Carlisle railway)

It began to snow shortly after noon. Heavy grey clouds settled on the Pennines where Ingleborough nods at Penyghent across Chapel-le-dale, and the first venturesome flakes swirled towards the sodden ground. Soon there was a thin white blanket on the fields, the topstones of the walls which in this part of Yorkshire pattern the fells like the web of a giant spider, and the narrow, puddly road from Ingleton to Hawes. The farmers did not mind the snow, for their barns were packed with hay and the cattle were comfortably installed in the shippons. They had taken the precaution of rounding up the sheep. Then they settled behind grey walls a yard thick and toasted their feet at the peat fire, watching the tiny mauve and blue flames rippling over the heavy brown turves.

At Ribblehead, however, there were men and women who shuddered at the prospect of deep drifts, for here the work of building the railway between Settle and Carlisle was being pressed forward with great speed. The stumps of masonry that would eventually form the legs of the huge viaduct designed to take the tracks across the valley to Blea Moor were growing daily within a web of scaffolding. The navvies came from all parts of the country, lured by high wages and steady employment for several years, but they uttered hard words against the weather with its wild contrasts between drought and deep snow, its sudden furious thunderstorms and biting winds. Now, on this Christmas Eve of 1873, they steeled themselves for another phase of bitter weather, and not even the prospects of festivity and hard drinking could quite chase from their minds the gloom of snowtime.

Half past five, and work for the day ended. Hundreds of men trudged home through the mud of Batty Green, through the reeds and bents, to the huts they temporarily called home. The shanty town sprawled over acres of ground, made up of wooden buildings, covered with black felting, which had been set down haphazardly on the slope above the river head, though there were other roughly-constructed dwellings as well, from old caravans to hovels which would have made the early cave dwellers shudder.

Henry Pullen made for a hut, at the gable of which stood a tall caravan, threw open the wooden door, carefully wiped his feet on sacking laid on the floor, and gratefully sought out the warmth of the fire, on which coal spluttered and smoked. Six navvies followed him into the house, for Mrs. Pullen had shrewdly arranged good accommodation with the object of taking in lodgers. The navvies vanished into their own quarters, and Henry Pullen greeted his wife and two daughters.

Mrs. Pullen was a huge woman in every sense – huge of frame and huge of disposition: robust, powerful, purposeful, but also with a genuine kindliness of heart which casual acquaintances never met. The daughters were aged twenty and fourteen, the elder being an extremely pretty girl who held the eyes of the navvies as she wandered through the "town". This cheerful, independent family had never known a stone house for years and had always followed in the wake of the railway builders. Christmas Eve was for them the time of celebration, and in the room were home-made paper streamers, a small conifer tree, its feet in a bucket, and sprigs of holly, which peeped from behind the wall decorations.

Washed and fed, Henry Pullen felt a new man. He settled himself by the fire, the steam of a clay pipe between his lips, and sighed with contentment. From the room occupied by the navvies came the squeaking of a violin, as though it were being dragged round the floor rather than played, and soon came a polite tap on the communicating door.

"Come in," yelled Mrs. Pullen, and into the room tramped a navvy, blushing from ear to ear but with a sparkle in his eyes. He "desired that the navvy brotherhood might join in the celebrations". They would conduct themselves with restraint – and bring some "liquid cheer" as well as music.

"Aye, come in, lads," said Henry Pullen. Mrs. Pullen only stipulated for order. The navvies trooped quietly in and settled shyly on the edge of a form. They were given glasses of wine, and then the black-eyed leader whispered something in Mrs. Pullen's ear. He slipped into the next room and returned with a bucket of strong ale and a bottle of whiskey.

The fiddler ran the bow over the taut strings, and a smart, ruddy-faced young fellow, Jack Pegton by name, promptly sang "Good King Wenceslas". Soon the party was in full swing, with chatter and community singing. The streamers seemed to flutter with the draught from a dozen mouths. There was a dance – something between a reel and an Irish jig – which set the floor boards creaking, and one of the lasses rendered another carol. But it was not silent for long. There was a loud rap on the door. Mrs. Pullen admitted a stranger – a navvy in working dress, with arm muscles like bands of steel. He introduced himself as the "Wellington Pincer". He was quite drunk, finding it difficult even to pronounce the Christmas greeting.

"Pincer" was one of the misfits of Batty Wife Hole, a man with a temper and an ungracious manner who was always picking quarrels in the hope of showing off his strength, and the navvies who had been enjoying themselves up to that moment were ill at ease. The Christmas spirit did not permit Mrs. Pullen to turn him away, and "Pincer" stayed, within easy distance of the ale, making himself a nuisance.

Mrs. Pullen busied herself preparing a meal. "Pincer" grew louder and more annoying until, with three bold strides, the lady of the house grasped him by the neck, propelled him to the door and hurled him into the darkness. His strength was of no avail, for he was held in a vice-like grip, but she would not permit the other navvies to follow and settle a dozen old quarrels. The party continued. The old atmosphere returned. But then the "Pincer" returned, through a door which had been left unbolted. He was repentant, and pleaded to be allowed to remain. So once again he joined in the revelry – and the ale – until sweeping his huge fist through the air, he caught one of the navvies a fearful blow in the eye.

The navvy restrained his impulses. The quarrel would keep until after Christmas, and he must not brawl in front of women, but Mrs. Pullen was on "Pincer" once again. With the strength of four she dragged him across the room, hurled him into the snow and bolted the door, profiting from the last lesson. The "Pincer" was still a nuisance. He hammered on the door and shutters. He thumped on the walls, until something drastic must be done. Henry Pullen rose slowly to his feet and, in a gentle voice, called for "Joe" – a huge, broad-chested bulldog which was busy gnawing bones in a corner. Joe was released into the night. There was the dull thud of a heavy fall, a scream, some gurglings, and Henry Pullen called his dog home. It returned to the room, wagging its tail, very pleased with itself. "Pincer" staggered off, his clothes torn and arm bleeding.

The Christmas celebrations continued. As the snow swirled to the earth and built itself up into a thick blanket on which the wind would later prey, the sound of hearty voices rose from the huts of Batty Wife Hole, and for a few hours the grimness of railway building was forgotten, dominated by the old magic of the Christmas season.

John Priestley (1955)

15

KESMAS TAHME

'E days gone by, did t'women put
Plums ee plum-pudden?
Did tha mak it a dough, an call it duff . . .
Tha must a put some funny stuff . . .
Intid Kesmas pudden!
E'stead a torrkey, tha roast boar's ead,
It musta been nowt bud fat!
Why, ard raither av ad a sup a broth . . .
As mak me dinner a that!
Tha clapped tord Yuke Log on tiod fire,
An sarved roond Ginger Wine.
Tord waites come singing ootsarde 'oose
Tha thowt sike deeins was fahne!
Tha drove ti parties we coach an 'oss
An likelins got stuck id snaw . . .
Or tha carried a lanthorn, an trudged
    throuh'd muck,
We bunches a mistletaw!
Ti them Kesmas was a merry tahme,
Tha knew nowt av income tax,
Ner V.A.T. ner 'lectric bills,
Ner onny other modern ills . . .
Ooor mortal Sowls, we terror fills . . .
At Kesmas tahme!

Florence Hopper (1978)

BEFORE THE LIGHTS WENT OUT

(In the Dalesman's *first Christmas number in 1939, Ella
Pontefract superbly evoked the pre-war seasonal atmosphere.)*

Christmas is one of the most satisfying times in the Dales,
even when the weather is uncertain and dull, and sunless
days greet one instead of frost and snow.
We remember a journey up Arkengarthdale a week or two
before Christmas. Snow on Calva and Fremington Edge was a

16

background to the picture as we left Reeth, but as we climbed out of the valley past the last farmhouse the snow still lay on the roads, and presently we were driving between a tall, white wall of it. As Tan Hill Inn came in sight we met Michael Peacock widening the roadway between it. For an hour we talked to Susan Peacock by the glowing fire of the inn kitchen, then we dropped down from the ethereal clearness of the moorland to the murkier softness of the Eden valley where the snow was left behind. Two or three miles from the inn we came upon a man hedging, slashing off great branches of holly thick with berries, and piling it in heaps for burning. "We think nowt about it i' these parts," he said, and he helped us to load the back of the car with it; and the holly decorated our rooms that Christmas.

We ended that journey in Wensleydale on a dreary afternoon with mist creeping down from the fells, and there was cheeriness and gaiety about the lights of Hawes as we entered it from Mallerstang. Tufts of cotton wool to represent snow hung on strings down the windows, and between them were tinsel and toys and brightly coloured Christmas cards. We have come down to similar scenes in Leyburn and Grassington, Reeth and Richmond. In all of these there are new shops with large window panes, but the thrill of Christmas seems to linger in the old-fashioned windows which the children must stand on tiptoe to peer through, and where the gifts make up for their lack of magnificence by their endless variety.

But perhaps our most vivid memory is of a visit just before Christmas to the performance of a Nativity Play by the children of Halton Gill in Littondale. The wild, rainy weather through which we made the journey seemed to accentuate the simplicity and ardour of the little group on the stage inside; the young Madonna, the Wise Men, the children of other lands. I think anyone hearing that play must for ever afterwards have loved the soft dialect of the Dales. There was one small angel, a chubby, rosy cheeked child with a beam of joy and goodwill on his face. We met him another day shouting in far from gentle language to an obstreperous cow, but the perfect cherub remains for us that tiny dales boy with a healthy face coloured by wind and weather.

THE DISCOVERY OF CHRISTMAS CAVE

It was the first Christmas of the war, with petrol rationing and all that. On Christmas Eve, at the *Royal Oak* in Settle, a rough-looking character we later discovered to be the local poacher was talking to me at the bar, and offered me a drink!

"Tha's a potoiler arn't tha?"

I said I was, and wondered if we had perhaps got a rather elderly recruit to our potholing club. We had to make do with lady potholers in the war years; the chaps were all elsewhere.

"I've lost mi ferret down an oil."

There was a snort of laughter from Harry, my caving pal, and suppressed giggles from the girls. Ferrets fitted rabbit holes; I did not.

"What makes you think I'd fit a rabbit hole?" I asked with a smile, puffing myself out.

"Na, tha's got me wrong. This 'ere's an oil that furrit's gone inta after a rabbit, but t'aint a rabbit oil. Well t'wor wen furrit went in, but t'aint now."

"What ever do you mean? Wern't a rabbit hole, but t'aint now?" The others loved it, and the old chap looked more embarrassed than ever.

"I digged it, an' it's inta one of these 'ere potoils."

"A pothole? Tell us more." Ears pricked up. Even lazy Harry stopped smirking. The cave was on Giggleswick Scar, and I had visions of another Victoria Cave – found by a dog vanishing into a hole, if you remember. The idea of another archaeological site of this sort was intriguing.

He told us all about it, and gave so good a description of where it was in the wood above the ebbing and flowing well that we found it straight away next morning while working up an appetite for Christmas dinner at the *Oak*.

There were three of us. Jean, the schoolteacher, lost interest in the cave when she saw a red squirrel at a drey in the trees. Dorothy followed me into the very tight squeeze of a hole dug into the steep slope by the poacher, and we were in a pleasant little cave with stalactites hanging from the roof, barely six feet from the open hillside. They were the nearest stalactites to daylight I had ever seen.

In among the boulders was a half-eaten rabbit and a very fat ferret, its pink eyes and twitching nose blinking in the torch beam. Elsewhere in the cave were two more rabbits which later became a tasty addition to our sparse wartime diet.

How we got the ferret out I don't remember, but we were in our non-potholing clothes, and I found the only way to control the lively beast – it gave me a bite with teeth like hypodermic needles – was to truss it up in a handkerchief. After blocking up the cave, to save the all-too-vulnerable formations, I buttoned the helpless beast into my coat and set off to Settle.

We arrived back just as they were sitting down to the Christmas dinner. There was barely time to wash our hands and tidy up, and nothing I could do about the ferret except tuck it in my coat and hope no one would notice. I sat down a bit late for lunch.

No one did notice. Dorothy and Jean, fortunately, went to another table and I found myself sitting opposite Harry with a lady on either side. Their noses soon screwed up and they tried to move as far away as they decently could. Have you ever smelt ferret? They obviously thought it was me, and even Harry noticed it and made some remark about the ventilation.

I was about the last to be served. Just as the waitress was putting the soup down, the ferret, handkerchief round its neck, escaped on to the table. There was a screech from the waitress and the soup went over me and, next minute, pandemonium as the frightened creature rushed along the table, dived off on to a lady's lap and on to the floor. Someone yelled: "It's a rat!" More screams resounded and soup was upset.

The creature was eventually caught. The landlord came in and was surprisingly docile considering the facts. I was only too glad to part from the disapproving company and slink out, dripping with soup, carrying the struggling creature in hands bloody from a second bite. After walking round most of the deserted streets of Settle I found its owner and put the beast into an evil-smelling box with another ferret in a back-yard. Christmas lunch was over at the *Oak* when I got back. The waitress looked murderously disapproving when she saw me. I had not the courage to ask for some left-overs. It was the hungriest Christmas I ever spent!

We evidently did such a good job closing up Christmas Cave – as the cavern was named – that it has never been found since, and I have looked often enough. I remember it has possibilities of being extended by digging away boulders on the floor but we were not dressed for potholing when we went in, nor did we have the time. Some day, if they quarry away at Giggleswick Scar, they will break into it and the stalactites will be destroyed, plus my dream of another historic cave dig archaeological site.

The potholing club never forgave me, Harry most of all. At the *Royal Oak* we were regarded as a disreputable misbehaving "shower" and had to frequent another pub where the beer was not so good. Harry liked his beer.

R. Dove (1974)

A WARTIME CHRISTMAS

With true Yorkshire hospitality mother rose to the challenge thrown out by the Y.M.C.A. for households to invite servicemen into the homes during the Christmas period. It was 1942, food was rationed, but, living at the shop, it was a problem easily brushed aside. Mr. Schofield, the butcher, was more than willing to slyly exchange extra pork or whatever else he had for butter, sugar and tea extras. And dad's good friend the flour traveller had already managed to sneak in a sackful of real white flour under the cover of darkness. This was kept hidden beneath the double bed, and dipped into "for home use and treats". A wonderful change from the National Loaf.

We patronised a dressmaker who could concoct dresses and blouses, and that good old standby of wartime – the pinafore dress, out of material she had 'put by'. She also used old curtains, dyed a brand new shade and fashioned into clothing. There were packets of Pasha cigarettes to make up into huge musical parcels, the rare cigar or two given by commercial travellers – and we still had a set of fairy lights from the 1930s. Woods were scoured for armfuls of mistletoe; we'd need plenty all over the shop and house if glamorous, strange soldiers were to turn up! As for all successful parties, I made a list of games to be played so there would be no chance of "what shall we do next?" bleatings.

By jove, what a party! Knock after knock rang out at the back door of the house and shop on Christmas Eve. My school friends Edith and Jean were already upstairs waiting, with generous dabs of Evening in Paris behind freshly scrubbed ears. Piles of Spam sandwiches had been prepared and were covered with big white basins. Little pots of Colman's mustard dotted the starched white tablecloth, and dad's home-made ginger wine – though the only drink apart from tea and coffee – was delicious. Anyhow, who needed alcohol with such boisterously high spirits as mother always supplied? None of the soldiers had time to feel shy – they were immediately grabbed, kissed heartily beneath the mistletoe, then ushered upstairs to the front room.

None could have been happier if we'd been partying in the Waldorf in peace-time. Shrieks of merriment resounded as everybody tucked in at suppertime, the starched tablecloth fresh from Wiggan Lane Sanitary Laundry brightened with a few crackers we'd managed to find.

Supper over, everybody dashed back upstairs to continue the party. What a memorable scene! Twinkling fairy lights casting an almost magical glow over the linked khaki figures, and mother's black hair adorned with a band of tinsel she had found from our old Christmas collection – a cardboard box where Christmas tree baubles and the lights were stored up in the attic until the following year.

Addresses were exchanged, letters promised, airgraphs expected in the future if and when any of the assembled soldiers were posted abroad. Then the clock struck midnight. "Christians, Awake," struck up mother, "Salute the Happy Morn". All joined in, a teeny bit subdued now that our party was coming – like so many good things in life – to its inevitable close. But with hope in their hearts and new friendships made that merry Christmastide, all would go forth to "fight the Good Fight" and then maybe meet again.

Hazel Wheeler (1989)

OUR DALES CHRISTMAS DANCE

The treasurer of our Village Hall, a rather mournful individual with a mind like a cash register, says that the "golden age" of village dancing is over. He is, of course, using the word "golden" in its literal sense. During and immediately after the war you could be certain of raising a tidy profit by organising a dance. Now, young folk drive off in their cars or on motor cycles to dances advertised in towns and cities. And the rural dance bands have had to increase their charges until, as our treasurer points out, "tha finds thissen working for t'band, and there's nobbut ten bob or so left ower for t'funds."

Our treasurer is by nature a pessimist and his remarks may not apply to all Dales villages. Yet there is one dance in the village for which he can always raise a smile and can hire a band with confidence. That is the annual Christmas dance, known to the younger generation as "t'Kersmass hop". It was held the other night. If you had passed the Village Hall between 8.30p.m. and 1a.m. you would have seen light was streaming from every window; you may have heard the strains of music and the pounding of feet on the wooden floor, with the occasional yap of a sheep dog. The animal belongs to George Scarthwaite. By bringing it alone and ordering it to sit under a certain seat he can be sure of a resting place between dances, for the dog will allow no-one else to occupy it!

A small stage stands in one corner of the room on dance

nights, being erected an hour or so beforehand. This stage is occupied by the band, who can then be seen and heard by everyone and are reasonably safe from the swirling patrons. The stage was made after a band from Craggvale had its big drum punctured by a hob-nailed boot during a "Military Two Step". For this year's Christmas dance, the stage was occupied by the "Black Crows", from Shepley. "Aye, an' they sounds like crows," commented Owd Jeremiah as they struck up music for the first dance. But everyone knows that he can't abide modern strains.

In Jeremiah's young days a man used to turn up at the Parish Hall with his fiddle – "there were noan 'o these swanky dance bands then" – and when he'd been supplied with a glass of ale he would strike up a tune and play almost non-stop throughout the night. The men just left sufficient time to scramble into their working clothes for milking the cows next morning.

Jeremiah remembers one old fellow who was an excellent exponent of the fiddle but had a weakness for drink. "Between every dance he'd reach for his glass of ale, and by t'time t'dance was drawing to a close he wor almost out to the world. Funny thing, though, he could always fiddle even when he was merry. It seemed to put life into his tunes, though his legs were

ionicus

soa wobbly we'd to pick him up and dump him in an old corn bin to keep him upright."

For this year's dance there was a solemn-looking gentleman at the piano. This piano, by the way, has achieved great notoriety in the district, for many years have gone by since it was tuned, and constant thumping on its keys has reduced its voice to a feeble croaking. One or two keys have no voice at all. A pianist recently detected a jangling noise when he began to play, and found that several of the "strings" were loose. As the dance was about to commence he simply ripped them from their places! There is an excellent piano at the Hall, but this was given to the Women's Institute, who shrewdly had a lock fitted so that it could not be used for dances.

The pianist who had the job of providing music for our Christmas dance knew the instrument for what it was. He removed his coat – and the front of the piano – before performing, and for the rest of the dance a succession of cigarettes were burning either in his mouth or at the edge of the ivory keys. Someone brought him a cup of tea about eleven o'clock, and this was placed on the lid. Then a member of the Hall Committee removed it, fearing that it would fall inside and dampen the works. "Aye, we know 'at Beethoven were a bit sloppy wi' pianos, but there's no reason why ours should suffer any more," commented the man who is our Church choirmaster.

There was a trumpeter in the band, and he played long and furiously. The small children were fascinated by the way his face changed colour during the pieces, from a light pink to a violent purple. The third member of the "Black Crows" band played the double bass. A fourth operated the drums.

"It wor a lively do," commented Owd Jeremiah afterwards. And these words were echoed, in a monetary sense, by our treasurer who, for a few hours at least, had his confidence in the future of the village dance fully restored.

W.R. Mitchell (1957)

2

CUSTOMS OF YESTERYEAR

FORGOTTEN RITES

Christmas was once the only day on which it was lawful for servants, apprentices and the like, to play cards – and then only in their masters' houses. It may be recalled that Sir Roger de Coverley was wont to send to each of his tenants at Christmastide "a pack of cards, and a string of Hogs puddings."

A "Lord of Misrule" was formerly appointed at colleges and similar institutions to preside at this season over the revels, masques, plays and feastings. But he, too, has disappeared in these sophisticated days. We have a less picturesque "Master of Ceremonies", abbreviated as is our way to "M.C.".

There used to be a pleasant custom in some of the Dales on the eve of St. Stephen's Day (Dec, 26th) of paying a visit to the "coo byre" in the hope of seeing the oxen kneel, a remnant of the old legend that on this night oxen would kneel in their stalls in commemoration of the martyrdom of St. Stephen. Another rite, now almost forgotten, was that of bleeding all horses on St. Stephen's Day, to protect them from illness during the following year.

A less pleasant custom on the same day, whose ending is to be welcomed, was that of "Hunting the Wren". Why this lovely little sweet singer of the woods was so penalised I do not know, but men and boys would turn out and hunt a wretched wren until they killed it. The corpse was then tied to a bough, decked with ribbons, and carried from door to door to collect money.

Not many people in Yorkshire will observe the old rule that the New Year must be let in the house by a dark man, although there are some dale villages where this ceremony is still scrupulously regarded and carried out.

And how many know the significance of Twelfth Night? In the old days it was not until the twelfth day after Christmas that feasting ceased. For nearly a fortnight our forbears filled themselves with food, and on Twelfth Night had one good fling before getting back to normal. "Brawn, mustard and malmsey" was the traditional meal, for those who could get it. More important, on Twelfth Day all Christmas decorations had to be taken down, for to keep them up longer would bring bad luck. Nor were evergreens burnt in the house – that was equally unlucky. In Brough people used to gather them all together and burn them in the middle of the town to the music of the Town Band.

(1949)

HUMMING AND DRUMMING

There used to be a custom carried out of watching with the bees. This originated with the alteration of the style of the ancient calendar when watchers by the bee-hives at midnight were supposed to determine the exact time of the Lord's birth by the incessant humming of the insects.

Christmas Eve used to be celebrated in a peculiar manner. At 8 o'clock in the evening church bells greeted Old Father Christmas and children paraded the streets beating drums and blowing shrill toy trumpets. This was followed by the lighting of the Yule Candle, an enormous structure of tallow and wick which was supposed to burn steadily all through Christmas Day and if perchance it became extinguished it portended coming evil and misfortune to the household.

Dorothy Morton (1940)

THE VESSEL CUP

In my childhood Christmas did not begin several months beforehand. Only a week or at most a fortnight before the Day the two village shop-windows sported paper and tinsel decorations, cotton-wool snow sprinkled with "frost", and those stockings of coarse canvas through which their contents look so much more inviting than they really are.

27

The first forerunner was the Vessel Cup, not on a given date but sometime in December or, in later years, even in November. In our district it was a cardboard box in which a doll lay on cotton wool surrounded by holly and evergreens, and it was carried round by a woman, often with a child in tow. They were never from our own village, but strangers from the market town. A version of some verses from *God rest you merry, Gentlemen* was sung, and they were given pennies.

I thought that this custom had died, but was delighted to meet it again in the 1930s at Goathland, where an old lady from Whitby (Miss Cole, of Henrietta Street) appeared, shawl over head in the traditional fashion, and singing the same old song. This, she said, had been handed down verbally – as could be seen from *all your friends and kindred* having become *all your friends in the kinder-y.* The box-cradle had dwindled in size, and the sole decoration now was a few artificial Flanders poppies.

An older friend told me that in her West Riding childhood the Vessel Cuppers used a clothes-basket holding a really big doll, and sang *Here we come a-Wassailing*.

Ruth Hedger (1959)

SEASONAL DITTIES

"Wishing" on Christmas Eve seems to have faded out. It was floundering in the area in the middle 1940s and no doubt faded away in the affluent 1950s. I remember the following ditties, handed down from my grandfather to his father and then on to me, and recited with vigour by lads in the village.

On Christmas Eve the following was the favourite rhyme:

> Wish you Merry Christmas
> And a Happy New Year.
> I'm teetotal and I want no beer,
> A bit of spice-cake and a small bit
>   o' cheese,
> A glass of cold water and a penny if
>   you please.
> If you haven't got a penny, a ha'penny

will do,
If you haven't got a ha'penny, "God
   Bless You."

Another very old wishing rhyme was:

Wish you Merry Christmas and a Happy
   New Year
Pocket full o' money and a cellar full
   o' beer,
A great fat pig to kill next year,
An apple and a pear, a plum and a cherry,
A bit o' spiced cake to make a man merry.

Philip Markin (1972)

Though the Christmas spirit prevails, some ways of expressing
it are vanishing fast. For instance, the folk of the North Riding
used to say on 25th December:

Maay peeace, goodwill, an' gret content,
Be yours, good fau'k fra Heav'n sent,
May ivvery latter heeap'd up pass
Fra t'heead o' t'hoos, ti lad an' lass,
'Mang t'au'd an' young maay moth (mirth)
   aboond
Ez t'cup o' comfort gans its roond,
Beneeath thah theeak all join the lay,
Good luck ti all this Kessemas Daay.

(1954)

T'OWD TUP

Well over half a century ago, the monstrosity known as
"T'owd Tup" was walked round the remote Yorkshire
villages by the local lads at Christmas-time.
   It consisted of a bullock's head, with enormous horns. This
head, having previously served its purpose to adorn the local
butcher's prime Christmas beef, was begged by the village
lads, who attached it, in some ingenious way, to a monstrous
body under which walked two men bent forward to reduce

29

their height.

These two cleverly supported the body of the Tup, consisting of layers of stuffed sacks covered by a tarpaulin sheet. The effect was incongruous, looking far more like an elephant with an ox head than an outsize ram. Having succeeded in "shoving" the tup, with no little force behind it, through your front door, the leader of the company began by introducing it with a song.

After the song, refreshments were handed round in the good old Yorkshire style – mince pies, spice cakes, pastries of all kinds, oranges and apples, ginger beer and home-made wines. Then, after wishing everyone good night and a happy new year, the party proceeded to eject the old tup. Out into the darkness of a December night went the revellers, guided by the beams from bull's eye and stable lanterns.

It was sad news when, towards the end of the last century, I heard one of the men say to my father, "We're not cumin' ner mooar, sir, t'owd folks's deein' off en t'young ens thinks es we're not reight in t'eeard."

And with these words t'owd tup faded out of our lives but the memory of it will never die as long as we live.

Gertrude Van Zuylen (1953)

THE YULE LOG

The Yule log was brought into the house with much ceremony on Christmas Eve, and lighted with the brand of the previous year's log. While it lasted there was great celebration in the form of singing, story-telling and drinking. The burning of the Yule log is mentioned by Herrick in one of his songs; many were the superstitions connected with it. For example, if a barefooted person or a squinting person came into the house while the log was burning, it was thought that the coming year would prove unlucky, and if the log burned out or went out before day-break on Christmas Day, this too was considered an ill omen. The custom of burning the Yule log was prevalent among all classes, from the nobility to the peasantry, and the brand remaining from the log was carefully put away to light the following year's Christmas fire.

Barbara Mather-Green (1957)

Young Fred

YULE LOG

Ah've bin an' gorra Yuletide log,
As gurt as owt yer've seen.
Ah didn't chop it dahn missen;
Noa fear! Ah'm noan that keen.

Yer see, the're thinnin' aht i' t'wood,
An' Ah went up ter see.
The' sawed one up i' little bits
An' gave a lump ter me.

It tak's a lot o' trailin' hoam,
But Ah s'll gerrit theer.
Ah'm certain Ah can manage, nah
Ah've go' as far as here.

Me Mutther'll be fair capped an' all;
Ah'll tak' her bi surprise.
Ah doan't want thanks – not thro'
    me mum
– Ah'll settle for mince pies.

Will Clemence (1952)

31

3

CHRISTMAS SHOPPING

CHRISTMAS COMES TO CENTRAL STORES

O nce the Standard Firework's boxes were out of the way at our Yorkshire village shop, it was time to visit the wholesaler's to buy in for Christmas. I adored going with mother into town to Beaumont's Warehouse to wander round, after showing our "pass" proving we had a shop and weren't just the General Public. We selected garishly coloured Chinese Lanterns, fancy paper trimmings, balloons and a few Joy Bombs to put on view at Central Stores. Joy Bombs were rather expensive, some as much as 7s 6d even in the 1930s. I think mother really had herself in mind when she ordered those, but perhaps the butcher, coalman's wife or local doctor might buy one too.

Some were shaped like huge snowmen, with tall black hats

set at a rakish angle. I remember one of those cotton wool covered Joy Bombs was a caravan, and we kept it for years, filling it with small new delights year after year. We preferred them as a centre-piece for the table rather than any posh floral arrangement. It really was the climax of the meal when they were set off and toys, bracelets, necklaces and small Dinky cars flew in all directions.

Lots of boxes of crackers and packs of Christmas cards were ordered too, and all mother had to do was sign for the goods. Dad received the invoice in the post later; mother and I had the wild spending spree. One Christmas morning I found a huge cardboard box on my bedroom floor. When opened, it revealed a life-size cloth doll, dressed in a flimsy mauve dress with matching poke bonnet. I recalled having seen one exactly like

33

it in Beaumont's Warehouse, and I wondered if Father Christmas patronised them from Greenland too.

Some customers paid a small sum each week to ease the burden of buying selection boxes and other gift items outright. One huge deep drawer beneath the "fittings" in the living-kitchen was earmarked solely for Christmas goods "put by" for customers. Big selection boxes were half a crown in those days I think. Then there were chocolate cigars, with smart jazzy gold papers round their middles, and sweet "cigarettes" with strawberry pink tips to resemble the lighted end. "Smokers' Outfits" were very popular – how they would be frowned upon today!

Toy cardboard "shops" opened out to reveal miniature bottles filled with Dolly Mixtures and cashews. Tiny celluloid baby dolls with permanently fixed celluloid "quiffs" over rounded foreheads lay waiting patiently for Christmas Eve. Other favourite stocking fillers were French knitting sets, a wooden reel with four prongs on top, a hook to lift the strands over them, and three

or four small balls of brightly coloured mixed shaded wools.

Mother was in her element in the days prior to Christmas. In gleaming white starched overall fresh from the laundry, contrasting with her jet black marcelle waved hair, she looked far more desirable to the commercial travellers than any fairy on top of a tree. They breezed in with flurries of snow through the shop door shouting "Shop! Merry Christmas everybody", then opened their briefcases out on the counter to tantalise mother with a beautifully wrapped presentation pack of fancy Turkish cigarettes – "Passing Clouds" was one of the names I recall – or a bottle of perfume in exchange for a "smacker" beneath the mistletoe. That put the seal on convivial business relationships for the following year.

So many ordinary, un-iced, one pound Christmas loaves were turned out in our bakehouse that mother couldn't resist giving one to just about everybody in a surge of festive cheer. So each "rep" had one pushed into his eager hands, and customers who were known to be "a bit short of the ready" were delighted when mother took yet another from the seemingly endless flow coming into the shop from the bakehouse on big shallow trays.

"I'm sure that tray was full last time I saw it," Dad frequently remarked in a perplexed voice.

Similarly with the bottles of port, supposedly bought for Christmas Day itself. If any elderly, poor, or simply cold-looking customer entered the shop in the days leading up to Christmas, mother poured them out "a little tot to warm the cockles of their hearts".

The final hour before closing on Christmas Eve was hectic. Extra grocery orders to be collected, mothers and dads slipping in to collect presents for children that had been "put by". They smuggled them out in brown paper, hoping that the children would be too tired to begin rooting into "the groceries".

Even the best-kept secrets can go awry. Mrs. Cudworth, who had hidden little Audrey's presents at our shop, told us that once Audrey was in bed she had spread them out in the front room ready for filling her daughter's stocking. But Audrey, keyed up with excitement, crept downstairs feeling sick. Realising that everything was on view, her mother, without explanation, took off her pinny and flung it over the child's head. Then, guiding her into the kitchen, she administered a spoonful of Fennings Fever Cure and shrouded her head again for the return journey upstairs, muttering some lame excuse about draughts on the way up.

Yes, Christmas Eve was truly magical at our shop. None more so than the year I kept awake long enough actually to hear Father Christmas creeping upstairs. I heard him hiss, in a voice strangely similar to that of John, our shop assistant, "Are you sure they're asleep yet…?", then the growl of a teddy bear rolling on to the floor, and mother giggling somewhere in the distance… beyond my dreams. Pure bliss!

Hazel Wheeler (1988)

TURKEYS FOR SALE

Mrs. T always bought her turkey on the afternoon of Christmas Eve. She usually managed to get a good-sized bird for a reasonable price, at the moment when the butchers were wanting to get rid of all their stock. After all, no one would want to buy a turkey after Christmas.

Just before last Christmas, Mrs. T retired and went to live

36

with her sister in a small market town high up in the Pennines. The town had only one butcher. The two ladies went into his shop early in the afternoon of Christmas Eve. In the window was a sign that read 'Turkeys from £10', but Mrs. T thought that by now the price would have gone down. "Certainly not!" bellowed Hindcastle, the butcher. "Do you think I'm running a charity? You can pay the same as everyone else."

Mrs. T and her sister could not afford that price. They walked sadly across the road to Mr. Kindle, the grocer, where they bought their Christmas vegetables with a discount that Mr. Kindle always allowed for pensioners. Mrs. T explained their predicament. She must have a turkey and it was getting late. Could Mr. Kindle help? He thought for a moment, and said: "Don't worry. Can the two of you come back in an hour?"

Exactly one hour later, Mrs. T and her sister returned to the grocer's. To their surprise there was a huge crowd outside the shop and the people were blocking the pavement. Everyone seemed to be straining to catch a glimpse of a notice that had appeared in the window. It announced 'Turkeys from £8'. Underneath was some tiny writing that Mrs. T could not quite decipher.

Hindcastle came out of his shop, he looked puzzled and angry because no one was buying his Christmas poultry. He flushed red with anger and then turned as pale as one of his pork pies. Hindcastle reached the edge of the crowd and read

the notice. His reaction was instantaneous. A few minutes later a sign appeared in his window: 'Turkeys £7 each'.

The crowd crossed the road, attracted by the sign. Then they looked towards the grocers. That sign was removed and quickly altered. It now read: 'Turkeys £5.50'.

Hindcastle again altered his sign, bringing the price down by a pound. At that moment, Mrs. T and her sister appeared outside. They read the price, walked into the shop and asked Hindcastle's assistant for a large turkey.

Hindcastle had not noticed Mrs. T. He marched across the road, intent on finding out why Kindle, the grocer, had suddenly decided to sell turkeys. He pushed his way through the crowd. Now he could see the sign clearly, and the small printing that Mrs. T had noticed only a few moments before. 'Turkeys £5.50', it announced, in large capitals. Underneath was written: 'If you wait a few moments, they will be much cheaper across the road.'

Kevin J. Berry (1979)

DAD GOES TO TOWN

"Will the toy-shops be open
    to-day, Daddy?
    And may I set you part of
the way?"
> *The Christmas display will be on*
>   *show, Laddie,*
> *But I've hay to buy and a lot to pay."*

"I'll set you as far as the pasture gate
And jingle good-bye with the chain on
    the stile."
> *What toy would you like, you young*
>   *reprobate?*
> *Dad asked with a hint of a smile.*

"I'd like a wind-up horse and cart,
And a cricket ball and a bat."
> *And what'll they cost me, young*
>   *eager heart;*
> *My son, can you tell me that?*

"If you've anything left, please buy me
   a train,"
Then I took his hand through the wood.
"Good-bye," I called, as I jingled the
   chain:
And his answering wave told me he
   would –
He would buy me the town if he could.

                T. Bownass (1961)

CHRISTMAS MARKET

There is nothing quite like our market day before Christmas. This, the last and greatest day of preparation for the event, is almost as important as the festivity itself. Everyone contrives to be there. The buses are crowded beyond capacity. Inn yards are full of cars and gigs and carts. Every space for parking is occupied, and there is a great hustle of buying and selling, gossip and laughter, shop-gazing and bargaining. It is a sort of communal Christmas celebration which precedes the family affair.

The fun begins in the bus, for you may find someone has tied a piece of mistletoe over the place where the conductress stands. It is continued in the market place, where stall-holders crack jokes with their neighbours and with their customers, as if jollity, not business, was their aim in life. It bubbles up in the dining room of "The Brown Cow" or "The Three Kings", where over the farmers' Ordinary – which is an inappropriate name for an extraordinarily good luncheon – staid farmers tell stories that become more mellow as the drink flows more furiously. And it continues to rise and fall in waves till the end of the day when the queues begin to form for home-going buses and when neighbours and relatives are given lifts in crowded cars encumbered already by vast mountains of parcels and packages. Ours is a merry Christmas market day.

Christmas fat stock sales are not what they were. Gone are the days when butchers vied with each other to buy prize-winning beasts adorned with red and blue rosettes and carrying great prestige in the shops. Nor do great pigs lie somnolent in their pens until jabbed into squealing life by the sticks of prospective buyers. Yet there is still gaiety and laughter and bustle, with keen competition between housewives if not between farmers and butchers. There are the rival cries of medicine vendors and the sellers of pots and pans. And a sense of the romantic as dusk descends and the street lamps come on, and the shop windows gleam and every shiny car and polished orange and twinkling ornament throws back a sparkle of life.

(1955)

40

4

GREETINGS!

OLD-FASHIONED CARDS

As a child, and like most children in the early nineteen-hundreds, I spent many enjoyable hours sticking Christmas cards into a scrapbook with rather messy paste made from flour and water. So messy that my mother insisted on tying a piece of coarse harding round me to prevent me wiping my hands on my breeches. Looking back, I wish I had preserved that wonderful collection of cards, if only so that they would have served to remind me of many pleasant aspects of life in Victorian and Edwardian times. They were realistic eras crowded with potent memories, when material values promoted a sense of well-being – so different from the mad scramble and cut-throat philosophy some folk delight in today.

Christmas in those days held a special significance, and I think Christmas cards leaned towards a seasonal exuberance reflecting the humour and character of the times. I remember the Suffragette movement was a popular subject for Christmas card artists of my young days. But the fun-poking was done in the nicest possible way – I am sure that Mrs. Pankhurst enjoyed the jokes as much as anyone.

But the cards I love to remember are what I call "the old faithfuls". Many of them are still being sold today. The robin redbreast; the beribboned Christmas bells; and the joyous bellringers. Even the old-fashioned Santa Claus with the wide girth, and round, cheery face, dressed in jacket and breeches and wearing top-boots, and a black belt with a huge buckle. Yes, he can still be seen making his rounds by traditional sleigh or vintage motor-car. Perhaps you will be lucky enough to catch him with one leg down a chimney and an ever-so-bulging sack of toys on his back.

There is also the far from abominable snowman, sucking a clay pipe and wearing those hallmarks of Edwardian days – opera hat, striped muffler, and inevitable umbrella. I loved the tranquil pictures of snow-covered churches with lighted windows. Many of these church cards were published by Benjamin Fawcett, a Yorkshireman, who owned a small printing works and bookshop, close to Trinity Church in Driffield. He was responsible for those delightful folding picture books showing birds and animals in lovely colour printing. Children were indeed pleased if they found one in their stockings on Christmas morning.

Yorkshire can boast of several publishers of early Christmas cards. R.T. Barras and J.B. Blacket had a publishing house in Rotherham in 1868. Otley had the Yorkshire Joint-Stock Publishing and Stationery Co. Ltd. in 1860. In Bradford there was the firm of W.N. Sharpe Ltd., and J.T. Woodhead.

Time seems to have given these old Christmas cards a deeper meaning. I remember one of an old gentleman with wispy hair and mutton-chop whiskers, happily smoking his churchwarden in the glow of the fire. He, too, must have been thinking of the Christmases when he was a lad. And I was particularly fond of the crowd of rosy-cheeked youngsters wearing gaiters and tammies, tobogganing down the snow-covered hillsides, their fringed scarves flying out behind.

But there is one card to-day that I am always fond of sending and receiving – the Old Stage Coach. It requires little imagination to hear the sound of the coaching horn and the rattle of wheels over cobblestones; to listen for the driver's whip as he guides the swaying coach into the courtyard of the inn. The ostlers are hurrying to the steaming horses, and the coachman, so red-faced and jolly, shouts a greeting to the landlord waiting to welcome the passengers, laden with valises, gay bandboxes, geese, hampers, and other exciting parcels. There is something heart-warming about this card – even the faces radiate an atmosphere of good fellowship. With such a card we cannot remain insensible to the true meaning of Christmas.

Last, but not least, there is the picture of the carol singers. There they stand, in the soft light of a lantern, on the steps of the manor house, singing sweetly. They are, perhaps, children of the tenants from the estate. The door opens and a maid-servant beckons them in. The hall is bedecked with evergreens. They enter, caps in hand, to receive their largesse.

The Baronial Halls are no more, and few manor houses remain. Today Jack's as good as his master, and rightly so. But this simple card reminds me that there is something above material gain. That something is the token of regard for each other that existed between men from all walks of life at Christmas time.

William Taylor (1962)

CHRISTMAS CARDS

How curious is the Christmas card:
Victorian invention
To celebrate the birth of Christ,
Who scarcely gets a mention.

But see these sentimental scenes
With bogus yule-logs glowing,
And solemn robins wondering why
For them it's always snowing.

So once again, perennial chore,
We'll post out printed greeting,
And tick the everlasting list,
Mechanically repeating.

Until we reach a name we love
Through death, alas, deleted –
Or one who sent no card last year
And made us feel quite cheated!

For friendships are reciprocal;
We must be systematic:
They sent a card, we'll send one back –
It's neat and democratic.

And cards for folk we never see
Are sent with no misgiving:
Just once a year, a signed receipt
To show that we're still living!

You're right, old Scrooge, there's humbug
    here!
But, still, it's not too tragic:
We'll shuffle multi-coloured cards,
Entranced by Christmas magic!
                    Arnold Kellett (1982)

44

TWO YORKSHIRE GREETINGS

Mah Wish this Kessemas Daay

Here's ti thoo, an' all 'at's thahn,
Here's ti me, an' all 'at's mahn,
Maay all t'good luck, 'at luck can send,
Be thahn an' mahn reegt up ti t'end
Is what Ah wish, an' what Ah pray
Ti leeght on all this Kessemas Daay.

(1954)

Good Luck To Ye

Maay this Kessemas be t'happiest,
Mah lad, thoo ivver kenn'd;
Maay t'corrants i' thi pudden, lad,
Stan' foor t'joyous daays thoo'll spend
This Kessemas an' on thruff life,
Is what Ah beg an' praay,
Foor thoo, mah lad, foor thahn, mah lad,
Maay start this Kessemas Daay.

(1955)

45

5

CHRISTMAS DECORATIONS

THE TREE

The Old Man always provided the tree at Christmas. It's been a sort of family tradition ever since I can remember. He would come home one evening in the week before Christmas and bluntly announce: "I've a tree for you in the top pasture. It'll need decorating, mind!"

That was it. Us kids would grab our coats and shoot off to get the tree. We would cram holly into its branches, secure the trunk with a couple of ropes and march back to the house in a sort of procession, singing carols as we went.

One year the Old Man nearly forgot the tree. He left it quite late, in fact, until the shadows were beginning to fall on Christmas Eve. He walked into the kitchen and stood on the old mat, covered in mud up to his waist. "I've left you a tree

46

in the top meadow. I'd better be off."

So off we shot, armed with torches, lanterns and ropes. When we got to the muddy top meadow, we had a shock! It was a big tree alright, big enough to stand in the usual place in the hall and reach the second landing, but the trunk was easily three feet thick at the bottom and not much thinner at the top. In the middle, the trunk was warped and twisted.

"It's not even a Christmas tree," said our Dolly. "It's an awful ash tree – well, part of one."

"Oh!" said George.

"Oh!" said Helen.

"Oh!" said Matthew.

Everyone looked downcast, even Little Jimmy, who was only seven.

We kids dragged that big, ugly tree down to the farmhouse, and it took some moving! We spent hours decorating the tree, and it needed every minute. We trimmed the branches, painted the remainder green and stuck strips of green paper on them. Tinsel and baubles of every shining colour imaginable were hooked over the tree and Little Jimmy hung paper streamers wherever he could find a gap. We all agreed that it was the best tree ever.

We had just cleared away and were about to go to bed when the Old Man walked in through the kitchen door. His boots were covered in fresh wet snow and he looked to be dragging something. The Old Man dropped the rope he was carrying and stared at our freshly decorated tree. "But that's not a Christmas tree."

"Yes it is," said Little Jimmy. "It's the best Christmas tree ever."

"It makes the house look sort of warm," said Dolly.

"I hope it does," grinned the Old Man, "because I don't know what we're going to do for firewood now ..."

Kevin J. Berry (1982)

47

KRESSMAS TREES

" **G** ronnie Doy,* all t'other barns†
At Kressmas have a tree
Lit up, at neet, by cannel-leet
Please buy a tree for me;
Yan wiv a gowden star a-top,
Wi' siller' paper chains;
Shinin' balls o' coloured glass
An' tinsel like blue rains."

"Nay, Honey Barn, I'se thinkin'
A tree, I wean't buy,
Marry! I isn't fain to knaw
Them lile trees mun die
At Kessmas. Left i' Low Wood
They'd grow sa straight an' tall,
Happen for fifty, sixty years
Or more. They would an' all!

"Bonnier nor ony shinin' balls
Is t'gowd moon, thro' an arch
O' branches. Rarer nor tinsel
Is siller chains o' larch:
Sitha! I'll tak' thee Kressmas Eve
To woods wheer thoo can larn,
'At real stars twinkle on each twig
Like crystal, Honey Barn!"

Dorothy Una Ratcliffe (1952)

*Grannie Darling   † children

HECKMONDWIKE LIGHTS

D o you remember the "lights" at Heckmondwike? Do you
remember standing in front of the great Christmas tree
in the Park, seeing the toys with lights inside hanging on
its branches?

Coloured lights criss-crossed the streets and festooned the

trees. Cinderella's coach sparkled as its wheels went round on an endless journey, an elephant made a treadmill of a coloured ball and a butterfly hovered with brilliant wings in the night air. Children standing with parents absorbed the Christmas feeling in the clammy dampness.

The noise of the trams and the voices of the market traders still echoing in the late evening were all part of the magic. Earlier we had been down in the cellars of Porrits and Althams (shops long since vanished) to see masses of toys that Santa might bring if we were good! Santa did visit our home, although many were not so lucky, but we all shared the magic of the "lights".

The traders tried to draw customers and the market teemed with people until after 9pm. All this in the days of the depression when many pockets were empty. Money was scarce but there was never another place quite like Heckmondwike, so bright and bustling. A little town with its own local council and providing its own electricity. Perhaps the traders contributed to the cost of it all but I'm sure it must have paid off. Most of all, what joy it gave to us children!

Today's children will not have such memories; no effort is needed to attract customers and shopkeepers close their doors at 5.30pm. Santa is not the man he used to be and dreams have disappeared.

M. Walker (1989)

They're bonny, is yon coloured leets,
Aglow on t' Christmas tree,
While t'e'es o' t' bairns, an' t' flames o'
   t' fire
Is breet as breet can be.

Shop windows blaze, choch cannels
   gleam,
An' t' stars shones doo fri' t' sky,
Yet iv it all, there's some on us
Feels dowly – life's awry.

Aye, but, when times tiv us seems dark,
An' we ha' lossen t' way,
We mun think on, The Leet o' the World
Was born on Christmas Day.　　　*K.S.* (1961)

49

THE HOLLY BEARS THE CROWN

The Christmas carol most likely to appeal to a gardener must be "The Holly and the Ivy": *Of all the trees in the wood the holly bears the crown.* The traditional emblem of Christmas, the holly is the tree of seasonal colours. Evergreen, it brightens the winter garden. A heavy crop of scarlet berries contrasting with the purest white of the first settled snow flakes is beautiful, quite worth the effort of putting on the wellingtons for a closer look.

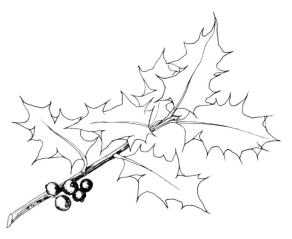

On Christmas Eve I collect the sprigs of holly – a little goes a long way. The rule for cutting holly is to take less twigs and branches than the holly has grown during the year. Cut each piece off smoothly at a joint or branch, and leave no snags which could die back into the tree as these will let in disease and rot. Carefully pruned to retain a natural-looking shape the holly will then be able to grow larger year by year. I cannot bear to rob the bushes more than this.

The carefully chosen branches are brought indoors to tuck behind the tops of pictures or fill the vases. A little piece is specially selected to be kept for the top of the Christmas Pudding. If the year has proved to be one that has not provided sufficient berries I brighten the twigs with tiny scarlet bows of red ribbon and drape them with lametta, to sway with the slightest air movement in the room, to add sparkle.

When I was a child my mother used to make a centre piece for the table. An old mirror was used to represent a frozen lake. This reflected some tiny models of figures skating. The whole was edged with a miniature landscape of holly "bushes" stuck in plasticine "earth", tiny fir cones and Christmas trees of conifer sprays. I always thought it wonderful, although I'm not sure how tasteful it may have been! I think the idea could still be adapted to make such a table centre, although the wooden model skaters may be hard to find.

A ball of holly, weighted with a brick, dropped down the chimney was the means of cleaning the chimney in days gone by. Perhaps Santa Claus could be persuaded to bring a holly with him to sweep the chimney on his way down!

Jo Makin (1988)

TRIMMIN' UP FOR CHRISSMUS

I vv'ry year, just a week afore Chrissmus,
We get t'haase donned-up at it best,
Wi Wesley-bobs, streeamers an'
    trimmin,
We've kept all t'year rahnd in a chest.

Ther's things 'at's called Japanese
    lanterns;
The'r like concertinas – but flat.
An' when yer pull at 'em to oppen,
The' luk like a wrinkled top-hat.

The' send me aht gatherin' t'holly;
It tak's me t'best part on a day,
Beside gerrin prickled all ower
An' loisin' all t'berries o' t'way.
The' say when Ah help Ah'm a nuisance:
Ah crush Wesley-bobs same as eggs.
An' allus get fast among t'trimmins –
Ah've hawf on em lapped rahnd me legs!

Will Clemence (1965)

51

ROOT AND BRANCH

I climbed a thickly wooded rise
Along a wintry Pennine Way
When through the trees, to my
   surprise,
Came voices. Then I heard one say:
"There's berries here. This lot'll do.
Hold back that branch, I'll hack it
   through."

Later I searched the spot and found
Mangled roots and rough-splintered
   wood.
Torn branches lay on trampled ground
Where a bright holly bush had stood.
Beauty laid waste – to deck a hall
Or bunch for sale on market stall?

E.M.R. (1991)

THE POOR MISTLETOE

If ever a poor shrub – and a half-hearted shrub at that – can
be pitied for the burden of all the ages it carries it is the
mistletoe. Alternately cursed by the gods for allowing itself
to be the innocent means of the death of Baldur, it was treated
as if it had hopelessly sold itself to the powers of darkness.
Then – at a later age – it found itself lauded as almost a holy
plant: or at least one that by its long association with the powers
of evil must necessarily be endued with power over those self-
same spirits. The quaint old custom by which the farmer presented the Yule-saved sprig of mistletoe to the first of his cows
that calved after New Year's Day, hoping thereby to avert evil
from the whole of his dairy, is a comparatively modern rendering
of this very old idea.

The mistletoe's curious manner of life – as a semi-parasite
upon certain trees – savoured of mystery, and its slow and
contorted growth was in itself a thing to excite suspicion. There

are still those who refuse to have dealings with the plant because of its unregenerate pagan past. Do we not, indeed, still ban it from our churches? But the majority of us are willing to risk any evil associations it may have and regard it in its more Pickwickian sense as a symbol of jollity. In these bold days we may no longer need it as an excuse for stolen kisses, but it still carries with it part of the atmosphere of the Christmas festivities.

(1953)

WESLEY BOBS

The Wesley Bob is the dialect form of Wassail Bough, and is used in all parts of the extreme West Riding. The so-called Wesley Bob was made by putting two hoops together, one inside the other, making a sort of skeleton of a globe. These hoops were entirely covered by coloured tissue paper, with perhaps a sprig of holly or mistletoe on the top, and the figure of a Father Christmas in the centre.

Before this device was thought of, it was customary to have a holly bush (in dialect "hollin"), with various decorations. The Wassail Song invariably begins:

Here we come a-Wassailing (or a-Wesley-ing)
Among the leaves so green

(showing that a green bough was used). I last saw the custom in 1893, when as a small boy I followed a group of Midgley girls who were going from house to house singing and hoping for money gifts which they shared. Hence the lines:

We have a little purse of stretching
leather skin;
We want a little of your money to line
it well within.

H.W. Harwood (1966)

6

SEASONAL FARE

THE FOOD THEY ATE

Our boisterous, hard-living ancestors did themselves well at Christmas time; their dinner tables abounded with every kind of traditional Christmas fare. Sheep and oxen were roasted whole in the olden days and were served on enormous wooden platters. Busy housewives were in their kitchens weeks in advance; chopping and mixing, weighing and measuring, preparing for the coming festivities.

In an old 18th century cookery book we can still read the

recipe for the famous "Yorkshire Christmas Pye" – for centuries it occupied a place of honour on Yorkshire dinner-tables. "Line a goodly pye dish with thick standing crust, and then bone a turkey, a goose, a partridge and a pigeon. Place the birds in the pye, so that the pigeon is inside the partridge, the partridge inside the goose, and the turkey covers the whole. Season well with pepper and salt, add spices, cover with butter, and seal with a lid – all save a little hole. Then, at the hole, blow into the dish a good blast of your breath, and suddenly stop the hole that your wind abide in the dish and raise up the crust, that it fall not adown."

Turkey was also long considered a Yorkshire delicacy. We are told of a young Yorkshireman, called William Strickland, who accompanied Sebastian Cabot on one of his voyages of exploration, and brought back with him from Mexico several large cages of these "most strange and marvellous birds". He took them to his home at Boynton, near Bridlington, and managed with great care and patience to rear them until he had established quite a flourishing turkey farm. He presented a turkey to Elizabeth Tudor, who so much enjoyed this novel food that she granted Strickland the crest of a turkey which is still used by his descendants in Yorkshire. When James I came to England he took a dislike to the boar's head, which had been the traditional Christmas dish for centuries, and turkey was substituted in its stead; it has remained popular ever since.

Next in importance was the peacock. Its skin and plumage were carefully stripped off before roasting. It was stuffed with sweet herbs, basted with gravy, and then sewn up again in its feathers, with its beak gilded, and its brilliantly coloured tail spread out.

Few vegetables appeared at these old-time Christmas dinners. Carrots, turnips and parsnips were grown and eaten only by the very poorest people who could not afford to buy other foods. Potatoes were brought to England by Sir Walter Raleigh during Queen Elizabeth's reign, but they did not become popular till some time later.

Jellies, custards and trifles date from the 14th century. When Edward III brought to London the captive King John of France, he allowed him to have his own personal servants. The French chefs taught the English cooks how to make these foreign delicacies with other sweet concoctions, and before long these novel "French dainties" were being produced all over the country.

Our Christmas plum pudding was a form of plum "porridge", composed of beef or mutton broth, sack, currants, and prunes, the whole thickened with brown bread and served as a soup at the beginning of the meal. During the "pudding age" of the Georges the amount of bread was increased, flour was added, and it stiffened by degrees into plum pudding to be eaten at the end of the Christmas dinner.

Mince pies were known as "shredded mutton pies", made up of meats of all kinds, raisins, sugar and spices. They were originally oval-shaped to represent the cradle in which the Holy Child was laid, and so became the subject to an angry controversy when the Puritans, who regarded them as idolatrous, ruled in England.

Pigs' ears stewed in ale, seagulls, herons, swans and storks, plovers, capons, geese and ducks, fried pieces of whale and "a good fat porpoise" all helped to furnish these old-time dinner tables. Home-made wines were freely handed round and the meal always concluded with the famous wassail bowl of hot ale, sugar, roasted crab apple and spices, piping hot in an enormous bowl. Our ancestors insisted that pieces of well-toasted bread improved the taste and hence derived the expression "to drink a toast".

M.L. Stollard (1970)

A VILLAGE CHRISTMAS CAKE

Those who visit rural Yorkshire during Yuletide know – or if they don't they'll quickly discover – that they are expected to "taste the cake" at every house at which they call. More than this they are, under pain of being considered "unsociable" and "uppish" if they decline, expected to eat generous slabs of cheese and drink home-made wine. Those who are entertained to this ages-old hospitality are critically watched and it is not easy to dispose of the wine in a handy vase or plant-pot, or pocket the cake.

Country clergy, who for eleven months of the year are the personification of truth and honour and to whom guile and deceit are unknown, frankly admit the Yuletide finds them "prevaricating" the moment they see a plate produced or a cupboard door opened. Rural medicos have unceremoniously bolted at the sound of a bottle being uncorked, and even the grocer's traveller, the insurance agent, and the lay preacher amongst the "chappilers", have been known to speak of stomach complaints and solemnly state that they have been told that plum-cake, cheese, and all home-made wines would have a bad effect on them.

The weak and inexperienced fall in what is something in the nature of an annually recurring Yuletide battle. Those strong of will, the prevaricators, the men and women who are armed against all persuasions, come through the contests not with honour but with internal peace. They may have flouted custom, they may have caused disappointment, and they may have laid a heavy weight on their conscience, but they feel their venial sin has saved them from a still heavier weight upon their digestive organs.

But at what further cost? They have according to Carthorne tradition, forfeited many happy months, outraged hospitality at an essentially hospitable season. More than this they have denied housewives of the satisfaction of hearing praise as to flavour, condition and richness of their cakes and the satisfaction of enumerating the exact number of ingredients, their weight, the type of eggs, the amount of spirit, the date of baking, the length of time the whole mixture was in the oven, the fears as to whether the heat was too great or not great enough, and how the result compares with last year's and the year before's cake, together with a comparison with the cakes made by neighbours, friends and others. The unselfish, the weak, the daring, the careless, the inexperienced, have said in their hearts, "We will eat and drink no matter whether we become merry or not and regardless of the result."

Now at Carthorne we have solemn, ceremonial, ritualistic, critical, and out-spoken cake tastings by a body much more competent than ever the official ale-tasters were of yore. Our band of old ladies (all knowing "what's what" in the way of Christmas cakes) who pay return-cake-tasting calls at Yule, sally forth as experts bound on a distinct and weighty mission. They wear their Sunday best and carry with them tea-party handkerchiefs to spread on their knees.

Though the season may be festive, the visit a friendly one, they feel that not until their verdict regarding the cake is given can they unbend, otherwise they may remain as frozen specialists who have "spoken fair to your face, rather than go behind your back for someone else to repeat".

J. Fairfax-Blakeborough (1951)

HOW TO MAKE FRUMENTY

Fifty years ago in the North-East of England, particularly in County Durham and in the Yorkshire dales, a dish of Frumenty was as much a part of Christmas Eve as hanging up stockings is to-day, and much more so than the still new-fangled Christmas tree was then in those isolated parts. While the children sat round the fire before going to bed father would bring in the Yule Log and mother would put the finishing touches to the traditional Christmas Eve supper – a dish of Frumenty.

Frumenty wheat could always be bought in the local shops around Christmas time. It is the grains of the new wheat, still in the husk. There are variations on the recipe, but the basis is equal parts of crushed wheat and milk and water, soaked overnight in a stone jar. It is then cooked for three hours in a slow oven with sugar to sweeten, till the Frumenty is thick and jelly-like.

1 pint milk, 1 pint wheat, 1 pint water
(sugar to sweeten)

The above is a useful dish to make. It can be flavoured with cinnamon or nutmeg, or honey, and currants, too, can be added. Stir these in just before serving and leave until the currants (if used) are soft.

Frumenty is eaten hot, with cream or milk if preferred. Fifty years ago the tiny hamlet of Stone, high up in Nidderdale, still had a curious custom connected with the eating of the Christmas dish of Frumenty. First the two eldest had to eat from the dish together, then the two next in age, down to the two youngest.

M.A. McManners (1961)

TWO CHRISTMAS RECIPES

Christmas Pudding
(enough for 4 large puddings)
Mix together 1lb chopped or grated suet with ½lb plain flour and 1lb sieved breadcrumbs.

Prepare 1½lb seeded (Lexia) raisins by chopping small and add 1lb sultanas, 1lb currants and ½lb mixed peel. Combine with the dry ingredients along with 1lb soft brown sugar and make a hollow in the middle. Beat up 8 eggs and pour them into the hollow along with the grated rind of one lemon and one orange, the juice of half a lemon and half an orange, 1 grated nutmeg and ½ pint of brandy.

Stir very well and pack into greased basins, tie down and boil for 8 hours. Leave some weeks before use. Steam for a further 4 hours before serving turned out on a dish with a sprig of holly in the top.

Yule Cakes
Take 1lb of plain flour. Rub in ¼lb of butter, margarine or lard and add 5oz of sugar. Stir round and make a hollow in the

centre. Work together 1oz of yeast with 1 teaspoon of sugar until it goes runny and then add ⅔ of a teacup of lukewarm water. Pour this mixture into the hollow, stir in a little of the flour and scatter more over the batter. Set to rise in a warm place for about 20 minutes.

Prepare ¾lb currants and sultanas, and ¼lb mixed peel. Warm ¼ pint of milk and add a beaten egg to it. Measure 1 teaspoon mixed spice and 1 teaspoon cinnamon. Work all these ingredients into a dough and leave it to rise for an hour. Divide into about 18 cakes and put them to rise for about 20 minutes on greased trays. Bake at Regulo 5, 375°, for about 30 minutes.

(1988)

TALKING TURKEY

Since the Second World War the turkey industry has been taken over by the geneticist. Birds have been bred for meat to such an extent that they are unable to mate naturally and are reproduced through artificial insemination. White strains were favoured, as the ingenious plucking machines leave a clean skin, whereas with coloured turkeys a mass of little, unsightly stubs may remain. The wheel has turned full circle, as there is now a demand for meat from the coloured birds. It is said to have more flavour and, as in the case of free range eggs, those with appreciative palates are prepared to pay for their fancy.

Numbers continue to rise. The UK's turkey population had reached 6,000,000 by the late 1970s, and over 9,000,000 by the late 1980s. Ministry of Agriculture, Fisheries and Food figures show that over 6,000,000 turkey eggs are now being hatched monthly in late summer. In July 1990 over 4,500,000 poults left the incubator houses, and 1991 figures show a six per cent rise. Along with this controlled supply pattern is a definite 'back to nature' move. Yorkshire woodland in the form of Forestry Commission ground is being used in a joint venture with Farmers' Glory of Newby Wiske, Northallerton.

The site is a conifer-clad slope on the Hambleton Hills, which takes 1,000 turkeys per 2½ acres. That figure is more than double the standard for EC-approved free range systems. The

Forestry Commission's North Yorkshire Moors Forest District covers 53,000 acres of doubtful profitability, and this turkey raising venture may turn it into an asset for the community. The remote larch woods are protected from foxes by portable fencing, and the birds pick up a proportion of their rations while being fed and tended by trained managers using fully equipped vehicles.

No antibiotics, no weight-enhancing drugs or chemicals are fed. The basic diet is wholegrain, and birds are fed under a similar "green" regime on each of the company's five farms in the Vale of York. Sales to city and wholesale meat suppliers are expected to reach 100,000 birds this year. Thanks to Forestry Commission co-operation, that target should be exceeded in future years. Farmers' Glory finds a demand for 'real' free range standards rather than for birds reared to EC minimum standards. The birds have that old-fashioned flavour and texture that older people miss, and youngsters have never experienced. These free range turkeys do take longer to reach target weight than their intensively reared cousins, and also need vastly more space. So Yorkshire forests provide the impetus for a £500,000 investment at the Newby Wiske base.

Edward Hart (1991)

GEESE FOR CHRISTMAS

Many Dales families kept geese. In Snaizeholme, "we kept five or six geese and two stags (ganders)." At Burtersett, a family kept a flock of similar size, and the birds nested in the back scullery. "Each goose knew its own nest!" Tom Thwaite, of Sedbusk, kept goslings for a month or two and sold them to men from the ploughing country to the east; the birds were fattened on the stubble. Swaledale geese were "crammed" with oatmeal or grain just before Christmas, for "a green goose was nea good." Came the time when the geese were killed, and when the family and perhaps some neighbours set to work plucking them. At Keasden, "some folk got the feathers off by scalding, but we plucked 'em dry, singed 'em wi' a blowlamp, then washed 'em."

Goose down was stuffed into a bag, which was placed in the oven, drying out the down and, hopefully, destroying any parasites. Goose wings were kept in bundles, to be used at spring-cleaning "for gettin' under t'beds an' furniture". In Craven, "we used to have a bundle of wings tied up and hung behind the cellar steps. Those wings were ideal for poking cobwebs from behind big pieces of furniture." The giblets of a goose were cleaned, packed in paper and pushed into the corpse, or giblet pie was made. A mixture of goose blood and oatmeal was prepared as puddings, and goose grease was kept for sore throats. "There had to be a jar of goose grease about for whooping cough, or bad cough in winter."

Goose was usually served at the main Christmas meal. "We went to our grandparents' house. A goose wouldn't weigh above 10 pounds then, and there'd be 20 of us – men, women and children." The only parts of a goose that were "wasted", indeed, were the beak and the webbed feet!

(1982)

7

CHILDHOOD DAYS

SUNDAY SCHOOL PARTY

When I was a child, the highlight of my year was the Sunday School Christmas party. We had to take our own food, then pile it on to the table. Some took jellies and others had fish paste sandwiches (lots of bloater; it was the cheapest). Having a shop, my brother and I were given lots of contributions to take. We couldn't have been more excited if we'd had an invitation to a party at Buckingham Palace. For Father Christmas himself would be appearing at this one.

The Sunday School party began at four o'clock. As mother

walked hand in hand with my brother and me down the hill, the orange sun would already have disappeared and I was secretly thankful for the warmth of my angora cardigan over my dress. It was a thrill to enter the Big Hall from the darkness outside for everything was festive. The Sunday School teachers had Christmassy looks about them and twinkles in their eyes that were not there on ordinary Sundays. Coloured streamers and Chinese Lanterns were everywhere evident and scores of balloons stirred gently from the ceiling. From a real fir tree hung shiny glass baubles, fragile and beautiful. We could see our faces – silly faces, with bulging cheeks and flat noses – in their orbs. Beneath the tree were blue tissue wrapped presents for boys, pink for girls. At the top was the glorious silver fairy. I was sure that she was real and that on normal, working days she dwelt with one of the Higher Ups in the Sunday School heirarchy, such as Miss Chinn or Superintendent Langley.

Long wooden benches were pushed together down the centre of the hall, and covered with starched white tablecloths. Waiting importantly were the thick white cups, saucers and plates. Food was set out on them as soon as it was unwrapped from the bits of newspaper in which it arrived. As there were no flies in December, the only health hazard came from the grubby paws and the heavy breathing that hovered prematurely over the feast.

We took our own cutlery, tied with cotton, our names printed on a bit of paper to save washing up. When we were seated, a teacher said grace, then all began chattering as helpers poured tea from the massive urns stationed at the tops of the tables. Some children ate only the insides of their fish paste sandwiches, leaving the crusts forlornly on their plates or pushing them beneath their neighbours. It was more interesting, if dangerous, to eat other people's concoctions. They looked highly coloured and slightly evil. Some mothers had even spread margarine. We always had butter at home!

At least one infant had to forego the pleasures of the table. After waiting all year for The Big Event, the actuality proved too much and this child had to be hastily ushered into the cloakroom to be sick. The rest of us went deadly quiet, straining our ears to listen to the awful retchings, which served as an odd accompaniment to the carols being thumped out on the piano by a Sunday School teacher.

When parents drifted in to collect us, about half past six, boys were invited to line up on one side of the tree, girls on the other. Then we all were handed an orange, a silver threepenny bit, an apple, and a silver-wrapped tangerine before going out into the frosty air. In staggered a bent figure in a red cloak and hood, with drooping white beard, ruddy cheeks and twinkling eyes.

I always walked back home staring up into the night sky, hoping for another glimpse of Santa, and maybe his galloping reindeer.

Hazel Wheeler (1987)

CHRISTMAS STOCKINGS

When t' last sound o' t'singers has faded
In t'calm of a cawd Christmas neet,
Then t'youngsters all sleep – but not
heavy –
They wakkens afore it comes leet.
An' then they finnds t'grand Christmas
stockings

A-hingin' on each laatle bed,
Near-brussen with bonny big parcels,
All tied wi' breet ribbons o' red.

Aye, then while their folks is still sleepin',
They oppens oot wonderful toys,
Wi' oranges, apples an' goodies –
Sike treasures them fost Christmas joys! –
Yet all yon fine things 'at they've gotten
Can nivver, nay nivver compare
Wi' t'Gift, born a Bairn in a stable,
T'world's life, wi' its burdens ti share.

K.S. (1963)

HAS HE BEEN?

About 5.00a.m. – me to big brother: "Has he been?"
"Who?"
"Santa Claus."
"Shirrup – go to sleep." This from somnolent bigger and older sister.
Another pensive thoughtful wait, "Annie can I get up to wee? – I really want to" – another anxious wait –
"No you don't – you're just being a pest."
"But I do."
"Oh well for Heaven's sake!"
So I scrambled out of the coat-covered bed to the bedrail and my stocking – 'cos that was my real ploy.
"He's been, he's been – look it's full!" – as I danced excitedly round and round.
"Shirrup, keep quiet, mi dad'll kill yer," says big brother.
"Oh dear," Dad's snoring ceased; and in seconds, "What the devil's up? – if it's that young un I'll skelp his hide off – gerrin to bed."
Grabbing the stocking I dived into my still warm pit and under the clothes conducted a stealthy investigation of enticing shapes.
Big brother: "Look I'll clip your lug'ole – keep still."
"But there's an orange and an apple and – and –."

"It's no good Annie," as he clambered out of our shared bed to shut the bedroom door. He then lit the candle in the fluted enamel candlestick.

Now in threatening tones: "Don't let the 'Old Man' (this was my big brother showing he was all grown up) hear a whisper or his belt will be round your backside."

So on a clipped rug under the window over the back lane, I emptied my treasured stocking – a big Jaffa orange, a beautiful rosy apple, a new shiny glistening penny and, wait for it, a chocolate smoker's outfit and a sixpenny book called "Piggy Pranks" all in colour. Pure ecstasy – nobody could be happier.

"Jim, could I just have a little taste of one cigar?"

"Annie could I?"

Brother and sister jointly, indulgently: "Yes, but only a little one."

Selfish me, I only glanced briefly at his Meccano set and her hanky box and scented soaps.

Fred Roberton (1990)

WANT TO BE A SANTA?

I was passing the job-centre in the middle of Bradford when I saw a notice, out on the front step and done up like a news-board. It announced, rather brazenly: "Father Christmas wanted by City Centre store – suit old age pensioner." I took a step back, obviously a reflex action in case my two little girls were with me, but thankfully, I was alone. Katharine, all of six years old, was going through the difficult phase of whether or not to believe in Santa but at the same time was not going to admit it, just to be on the safe side you understand. And she had been warned not to say anything in front of little Elizabeth.

Now I went through the wondering of just who Santa Claus was at the time of my sixth Christmas, and the whole episode left me ... a little bewildered. There was a dear old man in the village, Mr. Kerry, all kind face and fluffy white whiskers who always made me think of a garden gnome. I had not suspected him, even though he was jolly, ruddy and stout. About all I knew of him was that he grew vegetables like nobody else could and the lady-next-door to him, who was equally jolly and

Christmas with Old Amos

stout, had always wanted to marry him.

Then a new family came to live near to us and they came in and the man mentioned Mr. Kerry and his wife said, "Ooooooh! Isn't he a sweet old man. Wouldn't he make a smashing Father Christmas?" My mother silenced her, almost ferociously, and I was ushered out. But that conversation had set me thinking. Could Mr. Kerry really be the man who played Santa Claus at the Christmas Fayre? Santa's beard had always looked real and, come to think of it, there was always the smell of gardens about him. My Dad had said that it was the reindeer stables!

But Mr. Kerry was not going to be in the village for Christmas. He was taken away in the late summer to live at the seaside, and a strange anxiety crept into the grown-ups' conversations as Christmas approached. Two old gentlemen had taken over Mr. Kerry's cottage, but they were skinny, sour individuals who kept themselves very much to themselves. Even Mrs. Shoemaker, the lady-next-door, avoided them.

Then a number of the fathers, my dad included, started to grow beards, and on one Saturday morning, very early on, I saw that they had been been dyed white! Yet still the grown-ups were anxious, shushing enquiries from children about Christmas and getting very irritable at all talk of Santa's regular visit.

One night I stayed up late. I was reading until half past eight and, accidentally, saw a sight which young children are not really supposed to see. In the big house opposite, almost every man in the village was having his cheeks rubbed with rouge, and then in turn trying on a Santa Claus outfit. Each was being auditioned but Mrs. Shoemaker shook her head sadly after every performance. When Mrs. Shoemaker came out, I could hear her chuntering: "Aye he were a good Father Christmas. The best!"

There was less tension before Christmas. The men were suddenly clean-shaven again, except my father of course. Could I keep his secret safe from all the other children? Or would I blush with the embarrassment of it all?

At the Fayre, everyone said how wonderful the new Santa looked. He was surprisingly well-rounded and this jolly red-faced figure had a deep-throated "Ho! Ho! Ho!" I joined the long queue of children, hardly daring to look up and hoping against hope that I would not give the game away. But as my turn came

I noticed things that confused and bewildered me. Santa Claus had a sweet scent. Santa Claus had an old-gold charm bracelet and Santa Claus had diamond ear-rings peeping from behind bushy white hair! Santa Claus was Mrs. Shoemaker! She had even been to the seaside to borrow Mr. Kerry's bell and his big, black boots!

Kevin Berry (1987)

NO ROOM AT THE INN

Christmas time is full of memories for me as I am a long-retired school mistress. My favourite is from when I was teaching the carol "In the bleak midwinter". I then went on to the story of the Nativity and commented: "The innkeeper said he was sorry but the inn was full and could Joseph manage in the stable if he put down some clean straw? Joseph said he could and during the night the baby Jesus was born."

Then I asked the group of seven year olds if they had any questions. There was silence until one boy said, "Nay, Miss, I blames Joseph – he should a-booked!"

Yorkshire common sense!

Mary Burton (1989)

8

CHRISTMAS MUSIC

SINGING FOR THE CHURCH

I suppose it was Alan, the verger of St. John's Church, who was responsible for our carol singing episode. Calling one December evening at our local inn, *The White Swan*, he overheard us, the taproom crowd, singing Rugby songs. Being much impressed by the quality of our voices – or so he said – he invited us to join him in singing carols around the village on Christmas Eve. Readily we agreed and arranged to hold carol practices until we were called upon to sing in public. Alan supplied us with hymn books and for the following two weeks we practised nightly in the taproom to the accompaniment of a piano accordion, a trumpet, a euphonium and the constant clink of beer glasses. By Christmas Eve we were proficient.

As we assembled in the inn, warmly dressed and wearing gum boots – for it was snowing – we were joined by a gentleman who was known as "Cisco". He carried a banjo. As he could only play the tune *Ghost Riders in the Sky* we were rather apprehensive about his presence. However, as "Cisco" said, he would strum softly and as he was much bigger than we were, we agreed. With the arrival of Alan, who carried storm lamps, we set off into the bitterly cold night. With our heads bowed against the falling snow, we trudged to the village square where, after much clearing of throats and shuffling of feet, we commenced to sing our first carol:

> Hark! the herald angels sing,
> Glory to the new-born King.

The square was deserted and nobody heard our brave performance. Despite Derek's remark that people must have known we were coming and stayed at home, we sang on. After a few

more minutes our fingers were so cold we had difficulty in turning the pages of our hymn books. At this point in the proceeding a most peculiar sound was heard. It was a long high-pitched wail which rose to a crescendo and then died away to a mournful sob. Turning in amazement we became aware of a dark shape lurking in the doorway of a butcher's shop. The object of our indignant scrutiny moved into the light of our glowing storm lamps and proved to be a huge dog – a Great Dane. Opening its cavernous mouth it exposed teeth which would have done credit to a shark.

Nervously resuming, we sang another carol without further interruption. However, during our singing of:

O little town of Bethlehem,
How still we see thee lie!

the animal joined in again. Holding its head up to the sky, it wailed its mournful lament. Singing even louder, our musicians blowing their hearts out and "Cisco" strumming his banjo at top speed, we attempted to drown the dreadful sound. But to no avail. The dog's range of scale was higher and more penetrating than anything our concerted efforts could produce.

Eventually we admitted defeat and turned, waving our arms angrily at the animal. The creature bared its teeth and made a prodigious leap towards us. Panic stricken we shot backwards and fell in a tangled heap of arms and legs and musical instruments.

Gathering ourselves together we re-applied ourselves to the business of the evening and sang another hymn, *The First Nowell*. At the conclusion of the carol a bedroom window opened in one of the terraced houses and two small children looked down upon us. Shouting down, they said they had quite enjoyed our singing of the carol but we had not got it right and if we didn't go away, Santa Claus would not come. We said we were sorry if we had woken them up and delayed the arrival of Santa Claus, but it was, after all, Christmas and a time for carol singing. Where, we asked, had we gone wrong in our rendering of *The First Nowell*?

The children said they would sing the carol to us and show us how it should be done. We listened in reverent silence as their soprano voices drifted down to us through the gently falling snow. As they sang, other windows opened and more small faces appeared and joined in the singing, until the whole street rang with the sound of youthful voices. At the conclusion of the carol we applauded madly and asked for an encore. Unfortunately, lights were going on all over the place and irate parents were scolding their offspring back to bed. Politely they requested that we also did the same. Taking the hint, we moved on.

After walking some distance we began to sing again, until suddenly we were met, to our dismay, by the large shape of the Great Dane standing in the middle of the road. Growling it moved towards us. Shuffling backwards once again, we nervously carolled on, keeping a wary eye on our unwelcome companion. In this manner we paraded around the village with the dog joining in every hymn. Any pause in our singing would result in the animal rushing at us and driving us like sheep, back and forth.

Seeking some means of salvation we put our heads together and hit upon a plan. Under cover of our singing of *Silent Night*, we furtively made large hard-packed snowballs and awaited the chance to use them. Our moment soon came. The dog, now in full voice, its head raised howling to the heavens, huge paws crossed upon its furry breast, was at its most vulnerable. At the given signal of "Fire!" we hurled our snowballs with all our force at the animal, shouting as we did so, "Take that!" and "Buzz off!" and "Merry Christmas!"

Sadly for us, at that moment, a policeman walked around the

corner. Many of our missiles hit the dog, one more satisfactorily lodging in its mouth. Others, less well directed, hit the policeman and knocked his helmet off. There followed for a moment an embarrassed silence, during which the dog, tail between its legs, ran off. The policeman, after wiping snow from his eyes, face and neck, slowly bent down and picked up his helmet. Shaking snow out of it, he placed it once more upon his head. Taking out his pocket radio he spoke into it then advanced towards us, notebook in hand. He had, he said, received complaints about some rowdy carol singers who woke children up, ran about the streets like a flock of sheep and had a soloist who howled like a dog. There was also the matter of assaulting a police officer in the course of his duty!

W.H. Marsden (1975)

CAROL SINGERS

Children's off-key cheeky voices
Serenading Hobson's choices,
Carol singers! Not again!
God rest you merry gentlemen!

What a two-faced Christmas racket!
Out of tune, but well in pocket;
Doorstep duos none can quell,
Fingers posed to press the bell!

Hear their breathless, gabbled greetings.
Door-to-door their brisk repeatings:
Festive blackmail! Who could doubt it?
What would Christmas be without it?

Arnold Kellett (1984)

A SOUND OF SWALEDALE

Fresh from the production of a community play, using a large proportion of inexperienced actors, the music half of our writing team suggested the recording of a Christmas tape with local children singing carols. Not a choir, he insisted, just ordinary children enjoying singing. You got a natural sound, he explained, unsophisticated, uncontrived, genuine.

Our children and their friends were approached. All were keen on the idea. The lure of the recording studio with its likeness to a Mission Control centre especially impressed the boys. They agreed to practice the carols after school. Rod Hall arranged the music including descants and second parts for eight traditional carols; we would add four modern ones of our own.

Now, the difference between a choir and a group of children is that an established choir is used to set times for practices and the necessary discipline which goes with them. Our local children, my own included, had no such discipline. Instead of coming to the house straight from the school bus they would wander off to their own homes, ostensibly to drop off their school bags, and would re-appear at a time suiting themselves munching anything large enough to prevent the act of singing; or failing that, a good wad of chewing gum to accomplish the same effect.

They knew us too well, that was the trouble. We were not good disciplinarians. The children were tired after a day at school, but when else could we collect them all together when half of them lived in Upper Swaledale? Weekends seemed an impossibility, everyone had his or her own commitments. We struggled on, postponing the date for the recording; we were only half way through the list of carols.

We tried not to notice that only three-quarters of them were turning up. The best voices were usually absent. One afternoon, Rod continued playing his guitar through the splintering sound of a rock entering his kitchen via the window, hurled by accident from the hand of an errant caroller. We reached the end of the song but I had had enough. We would have to enlist help. Unsophisticated, uncontrived, genuine they might be but we were getting nowhere. An experienced friend agreed to help. "They'll probably hate me, but I'll get them to sing out," she promised.

We insisted on Saturday morning rehearsals and moved to the Methodist Sunday School room in Reeth, where all the children could stand in comfort. Yvonne taught them when and how to breathe properly. She instructed them how to sing the words clearly and to use expression. Rod began to look worried

76

they would sound like a choir, but there was no chance! He and his daughter went to record the backing tracks in Darlington using acoustic and electric guitar, bass, mandolin, flute and recorder. The sound engineer would add some keyboard sections. We were lamentably unrehearsed, Yvonne said, but if we didn't record the first half of the tape the following Saturday, there would be no time to sell the cassettes before Christmas.

Now, this is where the children came into their own. Practices they had not enjoyed. But the Real Thing in a Real Recording Studio was a different matter altogether. The endless instruction must have entered their subconscious somewhere. They sang for all they were worth – and again and again at times when there were technical difficulties. They didn't complain, they didn't moan, they behaved impeccably and the results were already being heard on the playbacks. They didn't sound like a choir, but natural, unsophisticated, uncontrived and genuine, came through loud and clear and, yes, also as though they were enjoying themselves. We were amazed. The following Saturday went as well, completing the second half.

The children's part was now over. We were left with a sound mixing session in the studio going into the small hours to balance the voices against the backing, producing a master tape which could be copied as required. We decided on a hundred. The first hundred were ordered before they arrived and several hundred more, subsequently. The tape had accomplished what it had originally set out to do – to hear children enjoying singing carols to lively arrangements. It remains a sound of Swaledale – natural, unsophisticated, uncontrived and genuine.

Felicity Manning (1988)

HUDDERSFIELD'S "MESSIAH"

Every year a tiny advert for a unique musical event is placed in the columns of the *Huddersfield Examiner* on a November Saturday. The response is always phenomenal, for it heralds the opening of a postal ballot for tickets for Huddersfield Choral Society's stunning rendition of *Messiah* – an annual tradition that has come to represent the corporate soul of the town. The ballot is a more civilised replacement in recent years for a West Riding ritual that used to see people queuing all night outside the Town Hall. At the ungodly hour of seven in the morning, tickets went on sale and just one hour later not a single seat remained unsold.

Normally held in the week prior to Christmas, one of the two performances of *Messiah* is for the public who clamour for seats year in and year out. The other is for the even more loyal subscribers – all such concerts have invariably been sold out for the last 150 years, although there is no truth in the tale that subscription tickets can only be acquired by inheritance! The faithful come to hear music of a standard so enthralling that it literally send shivers down the spine. They rejoice at the vision of their forefathers in ensuring that the Town Hall has acoustics far superior to those of many a modern-day concert hall. And they pay homage to a choral society that has become a unique Yorkshire institution.

In 1989, Dr. Jane Glover became the society's first woman conductor. I was privileged to be allowed to sit in on her final researsal for *Messiah*. Tall and thin, she used her whole body to conduct with quick and expressive movements. Such was her verve and enthusiasm that soon she threw her jersey on to the floor and almost danced round the podium. Members of the choir paid rapt attention, the men having pencils tucked above their ears so that they could easily make notes on their scores. Jane Glover's comments were firm but fair:

"A little bit more precision on the quavers."

"Some of you are getting a bit excited too soon."

"No hissing, please!"

To altos and basses: "Although you're practically sitting on one another's knees, you're musically quite a long way apart."

Then at the end she concluded: "We know we are the best

choral society in the world. But we must never stop trying or become complacent."

Rehearsals were over for a piece of music which she says has had a strong influence on her life ever since she first heard it in Lincoln Cathedral at the age of nine. "It is spine-tingling: the most astonishing musical piece of the year. Every number is a show stopper. *Messiah*, like the Huddersfield Choral Society, will endure for ever," she confidently told me.

David Joy (1991)

PASTORAL SYMPHONY
("Messiah", Handel)

And this can music do – it can transmute
Reality and Time itself to suit
Occasions.
For I have listened in a crowded hall
To Handel's "Pastoral", and seen the tall
Drab walls dissolve; the long cramped
   rows of chairs
Dispersed in starlight by the gentlest airs.

And as the strings played out their
    shimmering trills
I have stood alone on the wintry hills
Under Orion, with the cool clean smells
Of earth and wet grass roots round
    trickling wells;
Rich winter smells of loam and muddy
    lanes,
Of heath and snow and frost and
    ponderous rains ...
Breathe deep, breathe deep ...
And somewhere there were sheep, softly
    around;
Below, a village and the murmuring
    sound
Of water over stones; a farm dog's bark;
A lighted lantern twinkling in the dark ...
Of such symphonious blendings was the
    night
When Bethlehem shepherds saw the
    Angel's light.

Amy Jackson (1947)

9

ON THE FARM

THE MILKMAN COMETH

*Running a dairy farm and milk round in Denby Dale in the
1930s involved ceaseless toil. Yet one day of the year
was different to all the others...*

Why Christmas should be any different from any other
time of the year on a producer-retailer farm in the
thirties is hard to explain, except that one got out of
bed with a different attitude. Maybe it was the anticipation of a
celebration that made the difference. Checking the weather,
from the bedroom window on rising, helped to get one started.
Some Christmases were bright, crisp and frosty which meant
the milkhorse would need sharp studs in its shoes. Ice would
have to be broken on the yard water trough.

Maybe, on looking out, a foot or more of snow had fallen overnight and a path would have to be shovelled out to the mistals. A white Christmas, how nice and festive you thought to yourself as you pushed heavily stockinged feet into wellies. Maybe, just maybe, one would be lucky enough to find reindeer hoofprints and sled tracks in the snow. Before going out, a tap on the weatherglass clicked one's thoughts into gear. The pointer dropping to stormy was a likely forecast of more snow to come. Ah! but this is Christmas Day, this is different.

The routine might be the same, but one seemingly went about the chores with more purpose. The few tracks in the snow were evidence a fox had traversed the yard. Humming a carol as the mistal door was opened stirred the cows into action. Turning their heads as far as their stall neck chains would allow, they gave you a look as if to say, "What's all this about? – not heard this one for a long time." As the extra hurricane lamps were lit, other members of the family came in one by one, with broad smiles on their faces, calling out cheerfully, "Merry Christmas, I hope Santa was good to you."

Surprisingly, the chores and the milking were completed quickly. As "milkman" I went to change and have breakfast while the horse and float were being yoked and loaded. The larger churns of milk were strapped to the float sides, hawking cans in front, followed by the cream and eggs, which were packed into the box with a hinged lid, built across the front of the float. Butter was a weekly item.

The milkman was about the only outsider who was privileged to be in on the festivities of the family circle on Christmas morning. From the moment of knocking on the door, lifting the sneck and calling out "milk", the festive spirit was evident as the family chorused "Come in, Merry Christmas." Pausing to

knock the snow from one's boots before entering gave the children time to gather up their presents from the pegged hearth rug. After pressing forward to the corner of the table where the milk jug was placed, they would wait patiently while the milk was measured and poured into the jug. As the lid of the hawking can was lowered they would chorus, all of them at once, "Look what I got", or "Look what Santa brought me." A truly wonderful moment to share.

The man of the house, seated to one side of a cheerful blazing fire, would at this time offer a wee tot, "to keep thee warm on such a morning". In declining the offer, the answer was invariably the same. "Thanks, but no, there's still a long way to go." It was hard not to accept the hospitality, but it was never wrongly interpreted. It was understood.

A slice of Christmas cake with a sliver of cheese, served on a doily, was always enjoyable. Some households pressed a little "something" into one's palm accompanied by a strong handshake and a warm "thank you". Turning to take your leave, every good wish was heartily exchanged for the New Year. Amid spontaneous "thank yous and same to yous", one made off quickly to the next customer where similar joyous greetings were exchanged.

Towards the end of the round, on entering the kitchen, one was met by the most delightful aroma from most ovens. The bird was cooking nicely. This urged one on, in contemplation of the delightful meal and festivities waiting.

Prince and the float were not overlooked. A girl, year after year, tied a balloon to the lamp bracket of the float. A lady used ribbon, saved from the presents, to fashion a bow and attach it to Prince's lower hame strap. A sprig of holly was placed in the other lamp bracket by someone else. Another family fed sliced apple to the horse which had him looking for more as he started to follow them down the road. T'was the Christmas spirit.

On arrival home, only the essential chores were done. After unloading the float, the milk cans and measures received their routine wash and scalding. Prince was unyoked, stabled and given a feed. After drinkings and a change of clothes, a check was made of the mistals, stable, loose boxes and pig sties before setting off on the mile and a half walk to the family Christmas dinner.

James Lodge (1989)

83

HANNAH'S CHRISTMAS

Christmas Day is just another working day at Low Birk Hatt, in Baldersdale. This valley unfolds, endlessly it seems, to the west of Romaldkirk, beginning in the temperate zone of Teesdale and ending in the shadow of lean Pennine ridges which, at Christmas, usually have a crust of snow and ice. Hannah Hauxwell lives alone at a farmstead standing a few hundred yards from where the river became a lake when water engineers plugged the dale. It is not the highest farm in these parts but is, none the less, at an elevation of over 900 feet, where easterly winds can have a cutting edge like a blade of Sheffield steel. Hannah has been alone for 19 years. She is solitary, but not lonely, for there are human friends in the local farming families and chance acquaintances among those who are trudging along the Pennine Way. Non-human acquaintances include a sprightly dog named Chip, two cats and the few cattle around which her daily round, seven days a week, is organised.

During the week before Christmas last year, she tied up the cattle in the byres and resigned herself to the extra work this would involve. Hannah both loves and hates her cattle. She most certainly likes them, but is sometimes weary of the demands they make on her time and energy. She is now enduring her 50th winter at Low Birk Hatt, to which she was borne, from a nearby farm, as a small child. She has never liked winter, and often she dreams about what she imagines the Mediterranean to be like – blue sky, blue sea – as the gales pound her house, loosening yet more slates, and snowdrifts arch themselves against the buildings. Sometimes the wind whirls the snow in an action the dalesfolk call 'stouring'.

Last winter, the worst winter she can remember, left a legacy of work. Some of the walls that were gapped remain gapped. Some of the slates on the outbuildings are still deranged. You may recall that winter overlapped spring. The summer seemed pitifully brief, with the days apparently rushing by towards yet another winter. "Only the weeds seemed to thrive," she says. "It's amazing how *they* recovered after the bad winter."

No one called last Christmas Day, but there was a visitor on Boxing Day. Meanwhile, the little groups of walkers trod the Pennine Way and bade her good-day. Hannah has a supply of electricity, but last winter the power failed for several days. The cold seeped through every stone of her house.

"I'm not really a Christmassy person now," says Hannah, whose clear, rosy complexion speaks of days spent in the open air. Even on Christmas Day, she is absorbed by 'beast-work'. As she reflects on the colder end of the year, she observes wistfully: "I wish it was always summer."

W.R. Mitchell (1979)

TO A CALF BORN ON CHRISTMAS EVE

Cum, Loppy-lugs, ma bonnie cawf,
    Cum, frame thi sen noo, an' suck!
    Thi poor muther's nobbut dowly,
    An Vet aint cummed yit, woss luck!
Sitha, suck a sup o' thi bisslins,
    Sitha, yocken it, warm an' sweet,
Thoo mun fend a bit fer thi' sen
    An' stand o' thi awn fower feet!

Lig tha doon, then, on sthraw a bit,
    An' let thi mam lick thi feeace.
She's getten ower end, Ah see,
    Leanin' up agean skel-beas.
Ah'll tice 'er wiv a wisp of 'ay,
    An' fetch 'er a skep o' ceeake.

85

Thoo owt ti thry oot thi bellas
An' beal thi sen wide awake!

Sneeze! – That's reet – is sthraw kittlin
    tha?
Well deean! thoo's up o' thi knees!
Aye, beal thi 'eead off, ma bonnie cawf!
    Just leeak at thi muther's e'es, –
She's tellin' tha "Fend fer thi sen."
    Leeak'st tha, 'ere's a nice warm teat,
Hod up, thoo's framin', up thoo stands!
    Noo, suckle! There, that's a threet!

An' 'ow that poor maiden Mary
    Made deea iv a standin' stall,
Wi' coos all munchin' roond 'er,
    An' neea wimin there at all!
Dumb beeasts wadn't be mich cumpny,
    Bud wi' plenty o' sthraw an' 'ay
An' a soft cloot ti lap bairn in,
    'E'd be warm an' dry, Ah lay!

Clare Ellin (1962)

OUR WALTER

We were going to have Terry Wogan perform the Grand Opening of our "Barn Conversion", but "Our Walter" decided he ought to do it instead – no fuss, just nip in there and do it, not exactly quietly and not entirely alone, as he did have his four wives with him.

First I'll tell you a little more about Walter. He is quite a decent well-bred Blue Faced Leicester Tup Lamb, born in April 1986 to his mother named Betty. He made a fine start but unfortunately was orphaned at the very early age of two weeks, so he had to go on the "bottle". Because of this special attention Walter believed he was very important and for a while would not mix with the other lambs – after all they were only Half-Bred. So when they all went away he stayed on. We brought in four girlfriends for him, and he's had an enjoyable time looking after them.

Meantime we have been very busy converting our old barn into rooms for bed and breakfast accommodation. It was almost finished for Christmas, carpets laid, curtains hung and furniture installed. We decided to have a rest over Christmas and complete the other jobs later, then officially open the barn and be all ready for the coming season.

However, Walter had other ideas. On Christmas Eve at the crack of dawn he decided to take a stroll. He'd had enough of his field – it's Christmas he thought, I'm going to enjoy myself. So accompanied by his four wives he jumped over the wall and headed for the barn. Strolling around the building he stopped for a moment, and suddenly there was another tup just like him (he saw his reflection in a glass door).

I'm not having this he thought, so he charged. Bang! That's got rid of him he thought, leaving a trail of shattered glass. He wandered round the corner and lo and behold another tup. I can't believe this he thought – well here goes. Bang! That's got rid of him as well, another shattered window. On to the next; another tup, this one was made of sterner stuff. Number 4 tup saw Walter feeling a little tired but he did manage to get rid of him. He must have had a nasty headache by now because he actually missed two more.

We were going to have a day off on Christmas Eve, but first we would go to the barn to see if everything was in order. We couldn't believe our eyes. We thought "Vandals" but nothing had been touched inside. And Walter was just disappearing round the corner closely followed by his four wives, and of course he had left his evidence outside. Fortunately he had not been inside any of the rooms, but he had smashed two windows, one of them a patio window, and burst open two doors.

We called the window fitter. He could not believe his eyes either. He was amazed that this could happen to his windows; he told us they were burglar proof, storm proof, they were double glazed, but on the other hand he never said anything about them being "Walter proof".

It was very fortunate there were no guests in at the time or else they may have wondered what strange things happen in the country – is this how they greet you with your early morning tea?

We made temporary repairs, swept up the glass, fastened

Walter safely back in his field, slapped him and told him to be a good boy or else we would prepare some mint sauce. We then had the rest of the day off – well two hours. The insurance were awfully decent about it; they said it made a change from run-of-the-mill claims, but of course he must not do it again or it will definitely be the "chop" complete with mint sauce.

Let's hope his four wives produce something worthwhile in the spring.

Ann Foster (1988)

CHRISTMAS MORNING

The Christmas Story is essentially a pastoral one, and no one can appreciate it more than the farmer. On Christmas morning the dairy farmer has to rise early, because the milk-tanker will be early. His men will be away, but everything will have been prepared beforehand and by 9.00a.m. he will be able to go in for breakfast and the ceremony of present giving. He will go out again later, when perhaps a feeble ray of sunshine is slanting into the cattle-shed and glinting on the clean straw.

The farm is unusually silent. No tractors, no travellers' cars. Lying around, or quietly eating at the silage face or mangers stuffed with hay the cows seem even more placid and benign than usual. Moving slowly amongst his cows, along the calf-pens, and round the sheep in the field outside, no farmer can help feeling touched by the spirit of all the Christmas Days that have gone before.

I remember one particular Christmas morning. At seven o'clock the first suggestion of dawn was turning the cloudless sly above Carlton Bank to a luminous steely blue. Poised there, as though resting one fragile point on the heather, was the last thin crescent of the December moon. Close to it, very bright, was the Morning Star, Venus. The dark and frozen fields were completely silent. No traffic moved for miles around. An owl hooted from the wood, and as the dawn-light strengthened a partridge twittered amongst the turnips, that was all; a quiet prelude to a day of frozen brilliance, of cold beauty outside and warm cheer within.

Bill Cowley (1989)

10

GHOSTLY ENCOUNTERS

A PHANTOM HUNT

Many years ago when I was a G.P. in a remote Yorkshire village I had an uncanny experience which I have never forgotten. I had been called out to visit a patient late one Christmas Eve. The roads were icy and dangerous and as it was only a short distance away I decided it would be safer, perhaps even quicker, to walk. It was close on midnight as I left my patient's cottage. I set off briskly for home and bed. The lane and surrounding fields were white with snow. Frost shimmered and hung on the stark branches of the trees. The full moon was suspended in an incredibly clear sky.

The silence was broken as the clock in the church tower

began to strike midnight. As the last booming note died away I was startled to hear the musical notes of a huntsman's horn. The sound grew louder, came nearer, and now I could hear the excited cries of the hounds and the pounding of horses' hooves.

Down the narrow lane came the pack and the hunt led by Colonel Richards, Master of Fox Hounds. I drew back into the hedge to allow them to pass by, the hounds baying with the excitement of the chase. I felt the rush of icy air as they swept past. Then – suddenly – all was still again. Shaken, I continued down the lane, anxious now to reach home.

As I passed the village church something compelled me to glance over the low stone wall, and then I saw him – the fox. He sat completely motionless, bathed in the moonlight, beside a newly made grave – the grave of Colonel Richards, who had been buried that day.

Margery Ashton (1971)

THE "YORK MAIL"

Christmas Eve, and the first snow of the winter lay thick upon the ground. The sun had set some thirty minutes previously and the sky was overcast. A bitter cold wind moaned through the trees and blew the white snowflakes in small spirals as the grey light of a winter evening rapidly closed upon the scene. The "York Mail", a regular coach service between London and York, was already three hours overdue and its weary passengers were beginning to speculate as to whether in fact they would reach their destination before the morning. The guard and driver, wrapped in greatcoats, mufflers and scarves so that only their eyes peered into the gloom, cursed and lashed the horses as they skidded on the snow-covered road. Five miles from York there is a small valley which was wooded with oaks and sycamores; it was here that the strange events which befell this unfortunate coach occurred.

Evening was rapidly turning into night and as the coach passed through the last part of open country the isolated trees, hedgerows and fences all covered with snow, disappeared into darkness. Situated at the bottom of the small wooded valley and surrounded by tall oaks lay *Ye Olde Oak Inne*, a hospitable and pleasant hostelry for weary travellers. Feeling the cold and in need of refreshment, the passengers and crew of the coach decided to call at the inn for some ale and food before proceeding to York. Inside the inn, a large blazing log fire greeted the travellers and they were welcomed by the many people celebrating the season. There was ham and bacon to eat with the good Yorkshire ale and so it was not for many hours after, that the travellers decided to continue their journey.

When they came out of the inn it had stopped snowing. The sky was bright and clear and only occasional drifts of clouds covered the full moon, whose white light twinkled in the deep snow. Among the travellers there was a particularly evil one named George, who, upon seeing a poor beggar walk by, began to mock the beggar and throw snow at him. The others, being of similar temperament with the ale, proceeded to do the same until the beggar collapsed dead in the snow. Their hands raw with cold and their throats sore with laughter the travellers returned to the coach and went upon their way laughing heartily.

They had gone but a few yards when a terrible apparition came before them. In the road there appeared six figures, all a ghostly white. They had the bodies of men but faces of wolves and their leader was the devil himself. Such was the sight of these creatures, that all the travellers deserted the coach and fled to the woods. They ran so fast that some believed that demons possessed their very bodies. And those who did not collapse exhausted upon the ground in the snow, crushed their skulls against the trunks of trees.

The following morning a search party found the coach and all its mail and valuables intact. But nothing was ever heard again, in this world at least, of the six travellers who fled in madness from the coach, and all that was left to tell the tale were the deep footprints in the snow.

A. Marshall Horner (1968)

BRANWELL'S GHOST

At a little after 8p.m., the side door of Haworth Parsonage opened for a few seconds and the slight figure of Branwell Brontë slipped out to walk the few yards down to the *Black Bull*. There he found the usual six drinkers, each at a separate table alone with his thoughts. He nodded to them all and then took up his regular station in his own favourite chair. He had had it in mind to wish everyone "Merry Christmas", but merry hardly fitted the facial expression of anyone present.

Branwell passed the next hour in quiet contemplation, occasionally smoking one of his own hand-rolled cigarettes, or taking a pinch of snuff from the silver box in his waistcoat pocket. None of the other drinkers spoke. The noise of a gathering storm was overwhelming and somehow made speech unnecessary and tiresome.

The next hour passed slowly, punctuated only by the heavy, laborious ticking of a wall clock which had never shown the correct time in any of the previous 20 years it had hung on the wall. The following hour, all sixty minutes of it, passed in very much the same manner as the first. As did the next hour...

Moments before midnight the door was flung back, with such a fierceness that it crashed against the wall, shaking the dark stone floor with damp plaster flakes. A fierce gust of wind blew in, scattering some hats and woollen scarves from a table. Then a red-faced, wind-swept man entered. He made no effort to close the door, but no-one looked up.

"I've, I've seen a ghost," he spluttered, and he then demanded a drink.

"That'll be tuppence," said the landlord, without a flicker of interest.

"I've seen a ghost!" shouted the stranger.

But there was still no reaction from the other drinkers. The landlord merely turned to wash a glass, and then spoke. "Pasty-faced old woman with a lock and chain round her neck? Three fingers on her left hand?" he asked.

"Why, yes," said the stranger.

"Thought so," said the landlord. "Yes, she's a ghost all right. Appears regular every year at this time. Every night in December. She's a Christmas ghost. But as I say, she appears too often to scare anybody. Even the kids laugh at her. They throw snowballs at her!"

The room lapsed into its former silence and then Branwell Brontë got up to leave. He had an idea, for a "wheeze" that would certainly liven up the *Black Bull* and perhaps make Christmas in Haworth a good deal merrier than usual. Branwell

spent most of the next bitterly cold day in a hut behind the parsonage. His candles glowed against the winter darkness and he was seen occasionally in the open air cutting long pieces of timber.

Some time after dusk Branwell emerged from the garden hut, clutching his creation. It was a tall structure, rather like a scarecrow in shape, swathed in a lace-edged sheet of funeral white. Hands like bones of a skeleton protruded from the folds, one hand holding a dagger and the other hand a whip. The face was flesh-like and there were the realistic marks of fierce torture, and blood, the rich red stains of raspberry jam dripping from a socket that lacked an eye.

Branwell smiled. He took his splendid figure down to the *Black Bull*, and placed it against an iron railing where a solitary light cast an eerie glow over the ghostly figure and the frosty cobbles.

Much later on in the evening, almost at midnight, the door of the *Black Bull* was flung open by a very tired landlord and the customers reluctantly emerged into the dark to stagger home. Branwell was in the middle of them, his eyes closed in eager anticipation of the cries of terror – but none came.

For in the meantime snow had fallen, heavily, covering his ghostly creation in thick layers of white flakes. "Look at that," said someone close by. "The kids have been making a snowman! Isn't that grand?"

Branwell frowned and then walked home, wondering where at that time of the year he could find a toad to put in the pudding bowl.

Kevin J. Berry (1986)

11

TODAY'S CHRISTMAS

PANTOMIME TIME

Christmas time – and King Pantomime reigns again! We thrill on looking round a theatre to see the tiers full of happy faces in the light of sparkling chandeliers, and to listen to the animated chatter in the auditorium. Our nostrils are assailed by that peculiar smell of orange peel and stale gas.

Tuning up – what a glorious sound! Detected are the plaintive sounds of strings; the excited squeak of piccolos; the wail of saxophones and the twanging of harps, while the strident "A" of sounding brass mingles with the muffled dub-dub of drums... An immaculate figure appears on the rostrum and bows to the audience. A tap from his baton and the cacophony subsides: a wave, and the tuneful notes of a well-known over-ture fill the building. Another tap and the house lights grow dim: a sea of velvet rises to reveal a brilliantly lit scene of glittering splendour – and we are immediately transported into the fairytale Kingdom of Romance.

Cinderella continues to be far the most popular pantomime subject, particularly with little girls (as might be expected), with *Dick Whittington* second. *Robinson Crusoe* has a special appeal for boys, while *Mother Goose* continues to lay the golden eggs to everyone's satisfaction. Among the others, *Goody Two Shoes* and *Bluebeard* are seldom seen these days.

Although fashions in entertainment may change with the years, children of every generation remain loyal to the heroes and heroines of Fairy Land, and so the pantomime tradition continues, particularly in Yorkshire, where no Christmas season would be quite the same without it.

G.J. Mellor (1964)

RICHMOND'S "POOR AUD 'OSS"

The long dark nights of winter can be very frightening to small children whose imaginations run riot picturing weird and wonderful creatures wandering lonely country lanes. But the horse which might be encountered in lonely lanes around Richmond at Christmas-time, along with its attendant huntsmen and hornblower, is no figment of a fevered imagin-ation but a very substantial six-foot tall man hidden under an alarming horses's head. The real, snapping jaws surround a red plush velvet mouth, while great, black bottle-glass eyes stare out unseeingly at passers-by. Not a pretty sight to encounter on your way to the pub or, even worse, on the way home!

This "poor aud 'oss" is the leading character in a mummers' play which has been performed, more or less continuously, each Christmas for generations. Bill Ward, who takes the part of one of the huntsmen, is a member of a family which has been deeply involved with it. They have kept the play alive in the family even when it has been impossible to perform outside due to lack of a team. Fortunately ''oss' can be seen once again in the town as a team has now been re-established. Alongside Billy are two sets of father and son, two exiles who travel from Darlington and an RAF station in Scotland, and, happily, thirteen-year-old Jonathan, the son of Billy's cousin.

In 1989, merely as an observer, I joined the group assembled at Billy's house on a dry, mild night in late December. Finishing touches were added to costumes, top hats were decorated with holly and mistletoe and the Christmas roses and poinsettias adorning "t' aud 'oss" were given a final check, before we set off through the dark streets.

The first stop was made at a private house where a Christmas party was in full swing. The hornblower, an ex-trumpeter blowing a horn that once belonged to the famous Quorn hunt, announced the arrival of the players. The musicians struck up the opening notes of the song which accompanies the play as the door opened. The song tells the story of "poor old horse", who is carrying out appropriate actions, turned out into the open fields with only short grass to nibble. He remembers being in his prime, having the best corn and hay, and being ridden by his master in the hunting field. He is so weary he would rather die than live and proceeds to do so. As this is a mumming play he rises up again, death and revival being a necessary part of any such performance. The players were warmly applauded, drinks were proffered and accepted and then we were on our way again.

The remaining stops that night were at pubs, some close by and others further afield at Brompton-on-Swale, Skeeby and Gilling. It was traditional to visit all the local big houses on the tours but this has tended to die out. Billy remembered, in the not too distant past, performing at one of the local big houses where the guests were seated at a candle-lit dinner table and the staff clustered just inside the green baize door which led to their quarters, while children in pyjamas peeped through the banisters on the stairs. He was pleased that they were once again being invited to private houses, large or small.

During the early part of the evening, the horse was operated by an energetic eighteen-year-old who managed to prance up and down, even leaping completely off the ground at times, while wearing the top-heavy horse's head. Inside the head it is hot, dark and stuffy, with only a narrow slit to peer through whilst moving amongst the crowd, snapping open and shut those huge jaws by means of a lever. Young girls screamed and giggled, small children hid behind grown-ups, and even mature adults looked a bit wary as the horse picked off party hats, grabbed glasses of beer or snapped at onlookers. All this is not mere tomfoolery, however, for the horse has been considered a bringer of good luck and a fertility symbol since pagan times, hence the special attention paid to young girls. Later the horse was taken over by an older man and his performance was more subdued, less prancing, but rather more menacing as he stalked through the pubs.

From time to time someone would pop an orange or an apple into the horse's mouth. Billy's father never minded this when he was under the head, but he did object when glasses of beer were poured down its throat. Then he tossed the head aside and emerged, soaking wet, fists at the ready to take on the culprit!

Julia Smith (1991)

PRAYERS FOR SAMUEL JOBSON

We have a special service once a year in St. Anne's Church, South Cave, East Yorkshire, to pray for all good people, living or dead, known or unknown, who have loved and succoured the poor and needy. We pray especially for the soul of Samuel Jobson, deceased 1687, who in his last will and testament bequeathed ten shillings to several of his friends to purchase mourning rings, twenty shillings each to the neighbouring parishes of Ellerker, Broomfleet, Faxfleet and Brantingham, to be divided among the poor after his funeral, and his cottage and paddock to the church. The income from this latter bequest, at that time 45/- a year, was to be spent at an annual service commending his soul; the vicar was to receive 20/- and the remaining 25/- for white loaves to be dispensed to the poor after the service.

This custom has been faithfully observed for 280 years, and although the original 45/- has become inflated through time to £153, the main charity is now given to the needy at Christmas. This year we were a sprinkling of men and women, thirty or so children armed with baskets and carrier bags, and an intelligent terrier.

"Why is that dog barking in the porch?" asked the vicar.

"He's lonely and wants to come in."

"Can he behave himself in church?"

"Course he can!"

Two boys tumbled out of the pew. We heard them giving earnest instructions to the dog in the porch, and they finally settled him between them on the seat. They took the precaution of remaining seated throughout the hymns and prayers, each with an arm round the dog's neck. The dog gazed knowingly at the vicar throughout the service.

The vicar's wife handed each of us a loaf of freshly-baked Vienna bread, and as most of the children took a deep sniff and began eating there and then, another loaf went into their baskets to take home. Their mothers were out at work, perhaps as it was Tuesday afternoon and they were busy doing the ironing or probably just not the "church-going" kind.

It does not matter. The vicar in his wisdom knows, perhaps Samuel Jobson lying dead but not forgotten under the chancel knows, that although the poor will bless Samuel's bounty for a brief moment at Christmas, these children are receiving a gift fully as precious as the original intention. Many of them will cherish, long after childhood tastebuds are ruined, the memories of the delicious crispy taste and the smell of the long, white, Vienna loaves, shared with an intelligent terrier dog at "Jobson's bread service".

Pat Jorma (1968)

TOLLING THE DEVIL'S KNELL

Innumerable bell-ringing customs have survived in Britain, but none is more unusual or interesting than that which is observed on Christmas Eve at Dewsbury. Legend tells us that, in the middle of the 13th century, Sir Thomas de Soothill, who lived in Soothill, a section of Dewsbury, killed a young servant and threw his body into a dam. As a penance for his crime, he was told to present a tenor bell to the parish church of All Saints, Dewsbury. Every year on Christmas Eve it was to be tolled to remind him of his crime and keep him repentant. This bell was known for many years as the Black Tom of Soothill.

On Christmas Eve the old "Nine Tailers" or "Tellers" is tolled five times in sets of five. Usually this bell is tolled four times four for a man and three times three for a woman. After the old "Nine Tailers" have been rung, the tenor bell is tolled once for every year since the birth of Christ. Two reasons are given for "Tolling the Devil's Knell". One is that it will keep the Devil away from the parish for the next year and the other that, being rung on Christmas Eve, it will remind people of the religious significance of the festival.

The bellringers mount the worn stairs to the belfry chamber and take turns of about 10 to 15 minutes each to ring the bell. It would be too much for one ringer to do the whole job. They begin a few minutes after 11 o'clock on Christmas Eve and, tolling at 35 strokes to the minute, complete the process so that the last stroke comes exactly as the old parish church clock starts to chime midnight. Then the bellringers provide a welcome peal for Christmas Day, while inside the church the first communion service of Christmas Day is being held.

To ensure that the correct number of tolls are sounded, one bellringer sits holding a large pad ruled off into 19 large squares, each containing 100 small squares. As each toll sounds a diagonal stroke is placed in its square. When the knell is completed, the pad is dated and each ringer duly signs his name at the base, to certify that the "Devil's Knell" has been rung as required.

This custom has been kept up for hundreds of years as far as we can tell. It was absent for a period during the war when the ringing of church bells was forbidden except as a warning of invasion.

It was at this Dewsbury church, from 1809 to 1811, that Patrick Brontë was curate. He must have climbed the worn stairs to the belfry many times and heard the tolling of the "Devil's Knell".

Ethel E. Eastoe (1972)

100

On Christmas Eve at Dewsbury
They toll the Devil's Knell,
To celebrate Old Nick's defeat
And keep him down in hell.

A peal for every year since Christ
They cheerfully discharge:
Oh, pull those bell-ropes harder, lads!
The Devil's still at large.

Arnold Kellett (1988)

CHRISTMAS DAY –
SOMEWHERE NEAR HUDDERSFIELD

Wind howled outside, unseasonal rain lashed the terrace windows. Inside Edith and Walter, Cedric and May, and young Norman (aged 71) awaited the usual flatulence to develop after turkey and brandy-soaked pudding. Walter had got the £1 coin in his helping.

"Yer brussen, you," Edith comments.

"Brussen? Aye, damn near killed me!" moans Walter.

Disney cartoons on TV keep the lads amused while the women do the washing-up. "Easy tek'n up ent they!" says Edith as they return to the parlour. May agrees while opening the Teachers.

Cedric sits back. "Well ar kid, th's many as 'al noan be sat rarnd eatin' bird this tarm nex' yeear an no mistake."

"Oh belt up, yer morbid article. It's Kesmas!" May replies.

"Nay lass, s'reight enough," agrees Walter philosophically, "dista see t'paper t'other neet, baht yon Freddy 'Eskith? 'E's cocked it."

"'As 'e bi gum?" Cedric marvels, "weh, ah gu'a ta 'ell, a thowt eed bi cloggin' many a yeear."

"Aye, well. Fell on th'oil cloth thi seh, knocked issen art, nivver come rarnd. Whu ligged theer thre' days afore thi fun' 'im. Ah wuhra bit sluffed when ah seed it. Ee'd leave a bob 'a two tho'. Bye thi' 'eck, ah remember us goin' up 'is place a' th' aymekkin when t'owd boy 'ad farm. The'd no lav tha knos! Theh'd a buckit a'top a' cellar steps, an' when yer ..."

"Ere, our Walter, giv ovver," May interrupts, "wiv nobbut just

101

swallered us dinners!"

Walter though is unstoppable. "Fred wer barn' ta goe wunce, wi could 'ear this tricklin' an' t'owd boy, 'i sharts, 'Ere Fred, mek a less rackit carn't yer, aim darn t'sard when t'cump'nys 'ere..."

"Eh?...", Walter sees the bottle coming his way, "aye lass, ah'll 'ave a refill..."

"Well oss yer sen then an' get Cedric a pale ale out," Edith chivvies, "ah'm not yer lacky yer know!"

The adverts interrrupt TV. "So, gone 'as 'e?" Cedric thinks aloud. "What thi done wi' 'im?"

"Buried if ah think on, aye, 'cos yer knor, they 'ad family crypt up Slawit, an'..."

"S'weer ah'll goa, that, i' t'crypt," Norman announces with resolve. All eyes turn his way. "Up Awmbry, the's yar lot's up theer, s'fer three ahm cert'n."

Walter looks quizzical. "Wer, 'ooz in nar?" asks he.

"Well," Norman counts off on his fingers, "the's their Elsie, an' er Arthur..."

"Gerraht! Yer must be barmy!" Walter rocks with laughter, "yer'll nivver gerri' theer! Shi'll noan move up for thee, wuhra reight shiftless so an' so when she wer alarve wer yon...!"

"Ere you," Edith picks up, "wi'll 'ave a less callin t'deead."

"Nay," Walter concludes, "geh thissen burnt an' a' dun wi' it, ah s'all."

"Aye," Cedric warms to the theme, "ave yer ashes chucked weer ivver tha wents an' all. Ah wents marn ovver t'last furlong a' Yowk races. Wiv 'ad some grand days theer, am't wi kid?"

"Ark at 'im!" May rises. "What yer went ta guh theer foh, s'many a marl away an' yer nivver won a soo in all t'arms wi went. Well yer can put marn on t'sands a' Southport," May turns to Edith, "ah allus larked Southport..."

"Don't talk wet," Cedric chips in, "s'allus freezin' cowd n' blowwin' a gale theer!"

"Ooh, e's proper nesh this one," May goes on, "e's sat a' top a' fire t'day thru'..."

"Well it's reight!" Cedric forces, "Another Walter?"

Cedric waves the fast lowering bottle to Walter. "Aye go on then, yerv twisted mi arm!"

"Yer can't stall 'im," Edith warns, "an' watch 'im when 'e gets up, 'e'll bi fetchin' trimmins off tree."

As a pleasant haze overtakes the company, May hears a

rustle at the door.

"Ere, turn 'box darn a bit..." High pitched young voices are into 'Hark the Herald Angels'.

"Sithee – mummers a'r agate," says Norman, "bi choir lot frum t' Wesleyans."

"Reight, tek sneck off an' gerram in 'ere," decides Edith, "t'int fit ta turn a dog art tanneet, an' be a sart betnan all yon's 'arpin on abaht deein'!"

"An' we can gi' 'em a noggin, eh?" suggests Walter.

"Wi'll do nowt a't sooart an' 'ave the mothers rarnd 'ere creatin', s'enough wi' t'up growns lark thee gerrin' pie-eyed," Edith wags an accusing finger, "wi knors wheer thar woh a'Chapil Sundis..." She turns to May, "An 'eathen, ee is!"

"Aye – up Smithies' fields ah woh, an' it wer a sart 'ealthier an' all!" laughs Walter, turning to Norman. "Ah larks ta gerra goin' a bit! Gi' us bottle, ah'll a' one..."

A chorus or two later the young choir passes on its way, leaving the parlour still and quiet.

"Thee an' tha crypts after that, eh?" May breaks the silence. "Aye, meks it look reight... dunt it?' Cedric reflects. "'Nother drop, Walt?" he revives.

"Ah doant marnd if ah do!"

J. Stott (1990)

THE LAST WORD

Preparations were in full swing for the nativity play in the village church. Some local farmer had loaned the vicar a live donkey to add authenticity to the children's efforts and he delivered the same in a horse box which was standing outside the church.

My friend, Frank, was walking down the village street and asked a passer-by: "Wot's donkey for?"

"Oh, we got it for t'vicar," was the reply.

"By gum!" said Frank, "tha's got a good swop there!"

(1990)